LIMITS AND CONTINUITY

LIMITS AND CONTINUITY

TEDDY C. J. LEAVITT

Assistant Professor of Mathematics
State University of Arts and Sciences
Plattsburgh, New York

McGRAW-HILL BOOK COMPANY

New York, St. Louis, San Francisco
Toronto, London, Sydney

LIMITS AND CONTINUITY

Library of Congress Catalog Card Number 67-15426

1 2 3 4 5 6 7 8 9 0   B N   7 4 3 2 1 0 6 9 8 7

Preface

This text is a study of limits and continuity, and is designed
to supplement standard calculus texts.   It discusses limits
and continuity in several different ways, since students gain
understanding through comparison.

Continuity of a function and limit of a sequence are
introduced before limit of a function.   It is hoped that the
student will gain momentum while studying these easier
concepts so that when he reaches the difficult concepts of
deleted neighborhood, limit point, and limit of a function,
he will not lose sight of the simple pattern underlying the
limit.

Before we give the student many limits to compute,
we state the fact that if f is continuous at a point b in its
domain, then $\lim_{x \to b} f(x) = f(b)$.   If the student is asked to
compute the limit of a function g which is not continuous
at b, he may choose to extend the domain of the function g
to create a new function f which is continuous at b.   The
limit of this extended function may then be computed by
simple substitution.

For example, consider

$$\lim_{x \to 3} \frac{x^2 - 9}{x - 3} = \lim_{x \to 3} (x + 3)$$

The function $g = \{(x, y)| \, y = x + 3, x \in \text{Re}\}$ is a one-point extension of the function

$$f = \left\{ (x, y)| \, y = \frac{x^2 - 9}{x - 3}, x \neq 3 \right\}$$

The function g is continuous at 3, so $\lim_{x \to 3} g(x) = g(3)$.

The programmed exercises are, for the most part, less difficult than the text material.   We often introduce a topic with programmed exercises.   For example, Chap. 2 begins with a programmed exercise that is not rigorous.   Then we define function and sequence precisely and give further programmed exercises that are more demanding.

We have found that programmed exercises are efficient in introducing and fixing learning.   The student is prompted in the stimulus portion of a frame in such a way that if he reads carefully, he should be able to respond as the programmer intended.   As the book progresses, we use the sequential prompt; i.e., ideas from the preceding frames are used as prompts without rewriting them in the particular stimulus in which they are needed.

The student should be encouraged to write the response to each frame before proceeding to the next frame, as it has been shown that the student must actually perform a response in order to experience the economy of learning attributed to programmed instruction.

The author would like to thank the many people who aided him in the preparation of this book, especially John Otis, Warren Brainard, Alex Michalos, and Cheryl Phillips, who are really coauthors.

Teddy C. J. Leavitt

To the Student

Although Chap. 1 can be read without any knowledge of mathematics, we assume, as the book progresses, that you have studied the usual mathematics taught in high school. Since some of you may not have studied sets, inequalities, or absolute value, we have included an appendix that covers these topics. If you find youself lost, turn to the appendix; the material you need will probably be there.

At the beginning of Chap. 2 we have inserted a programmed exercise. Programmed frames are made up of two parts. The first part, the stimulus, consists of information that the student is to learn. The second part, the active response, is a statement of what the author expects the student to write in responding to the stimulus.

Cover the response portion of the frame, read the stimulus, and write your answer. Then compare your response with ours. We occasionally depart from accepted programming form and slip some information into the response part of the frame when we feel that you will be receptive.

We have enjoyed writing this material and hope that you will find it interesting and exciting.

Contents

Chapter One: An Intuitive Approach to Continuity

Some basic concepts pass unnoticed for centuries and then are exposed as great discoveries. Other ideas are known and considered obvious for years but take on new meaning when they are defined and explored.

When the caveman noticed the tracks left by animals, he observed that an animal with a heavy tail often left a *continuous* line between its footprints when its tail dragged along the ground. If the animal lifted its tail to the left, the result would be a *discontinuity* in the track left by the tail (see Fig. 1-1).

It may seem incredible that such a simple concept, taken for granted by early man, could become the study of great mathematicians; but men with unquestioned mathematical genius have spent their whole lives studying continuity and related subjects. In fact, after precise mathematical definition and redefinition, this concept has blossomed today into a whole galaxy of mathematical stars. Some mathematicians go so far as to contend that the burly modern giant known as topology is simply a study of continuity.

The mathematical concept of continuity differs from

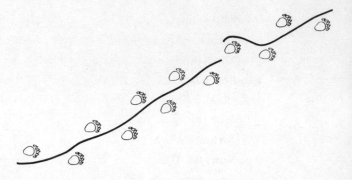

Figure 1-1

that of our primitive predecessor who, like some men today, would consider the flow of water down a river to be continuous. We shall consider this flow to be discontinuous. We have been conditioned by previous learning to think immediately of closeness between points when we think of continuity. The flow of water can be called continuous only if two molecules which are close to each other at the source *remain* close to each other. Therefore, the flow of water down the Mississippi is not continuous, since two water molecules which are close to each other in Minnesota may be separated by any number of means before they reach New Orleans.

If we are going to insist on this method of determining continuity, it appears that we shall consider nothing continuous. But, even when it looks as though we had defined and precised ourselves out of the possibility of finding anything that is continuous, there is still a great deal of continuity everywhere. The simple act of stretching a rubber band around a newspaper is a continuous transformation.

Two points A and B which are close to each other when

the band is unstretched (Fig. 1-2) are still relatively close to each other when the rubber band is on the newspaper. The stretching of the rubber band around the newspaper is called a *continuous transformation* of the points on the unstretched band (the *domain* of the transformation) into points of the band around the newspaper (the *range* of the transformation).

Now, at the risk of obscuring the simplicity of this idea, we introduce two Greek letters, ε (epsilon) and δ (delta). If the rubber band is stretched until it is twice as big in the range (on the newspaper) as it is in the domain (unstretched), we say "for every ε, there exists a $\delta = \frac{1}{2}\varepsilon$ such that every point which is δ-close to A in the domain is transferred to a point which is ε-close to A' in the range." We mean by all this Greek that if a point is within $\frac{1}{2}$ inch of point A on the band when it is unstretched, then it is within 1 inch of point A' when the rubber band is on the newspaper.

Why not speak English? Since we have been conditioned by previous writings on continuity, in which the

Figure 1-2

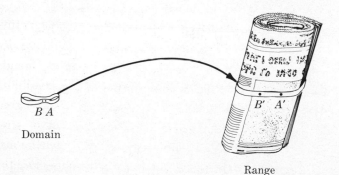

B A

Domain

B' A'

Range

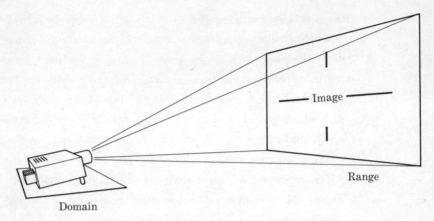

Image

Range

Domain

Figure 1-3

epsilon-delta language has been standardized, we find it more natural to speak in this precise way than to use loose nonmathematical language. It is hoped that the reader, upon completing this study will also find the ε,δ-language easier to understand and use.

Any correspondence between a domain and a range can be tested for continuity if there is a way to specify closeness. A slide projector is an example of a device which can induce continuous transformations. It projects the points of a slide (the domain) onto points on a screen (the range) (Fig. 1-3). Two points which are, say, 1 inch apart on the screen are images of points which are $\frac{1}{100}$ inch apart on the slide. Given an ε-closeness in the range, we can compute a δ-closeness in the domain, so that any two points which are δ-close in the domain will be ε-close in the range. We call this projection a *continuous mapping* (transformation) of points of the slide onto points on the screen. Here, $\delta = \frac{1}{100}\varepsilon$.

On the other hand, if we have a picture and wish to

make a smaller copy, we can devise a system of lenses (Fig. 1-4) which will project a smaller image. Again, any ε-closeness in the range can be obtained by specifying some computable δ-closeness in the domain. It is possible for two points which are $\frac{1}{100}$ inch apart in the range to come from points which are $\frac{1}{10}$ inch apart in the domain, in which case δ is 10 times as large as ε. Remember that in the first example δ was only $\frac{1}{100}$ as large as ε.

The important thing about both examples is that there is a way of *computing* a closeness in the domain for any given closeness in the range. It does not make any difference whether or not the points are closer in the range than they are in the domain.

We call things in reality continuous if they fit our model of them in a precise way. Continuity is an abstraction that does not apply directly to reality but to a model of reality. By specifying certain symbols to represent the domain, range, and transformation, we can decide whether our model is continuous.

The animal track that was considered continuous by the

Figure 1-4

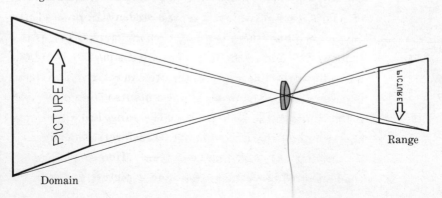

Domain

Range

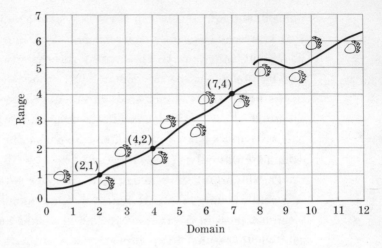

Figure 1-5

caveman is also continuous by the mathematical standard. We can define a domain and range so that points which are close to each other in the domain will be transported or mapped into points which are close to each other in the range.

In Fig. 1-5 the range is the vertical line on the left, and the domain is the horizontal line below the track. We shall consider the line made by the tail to be an infinite number of points, each of which is represented by an ordered pair (x, y). Suppose there is a point on the track which is two units to the right of the line representing the range and one unit above the line representing the domain. This point is designated by the ordered pair $(2, 1)$. The point $(4, 2)$ is four units to the right of the line representing the range and two units above the line representing the domain.

In Fig. 1-6, the points A' and B' in the range are thought of as being associated with points A and B in the domain, and (A, A') and (B, B') are the points on the track that represent the transformation of A to A' and B to B'. The point (x, y) of the track maps (transports) x in the domain to y in the range. The point $(7, 4)$ is on the track, so the point 7 in the domain is mapped to the point 4 in the range.

It is necessary to clarify just what it is that we are calling continuous. *Transformations* are actually the only things which are considered continuous or discontinuous. If we talk about transferring the points on a rubber band from one position to another, we call this transformation continuous because points which are close to each other in the domain are transported into points which are close to each other in the range. The flow of water in a river is discontinuous because two molecules which are close to each other in the domain of the transformation (at the source) may *not* be close to each other in the range (at the

Figure 1-6

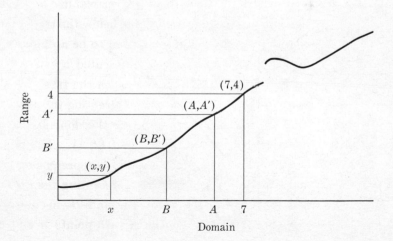

mouth). In fact, because of evaporation or other diversion, some molecules may not be transported all the way to the mouth of the river.

On the other hand, the graph of a river on a map may be representative of a continuous transformation of points in the domain (longitude) to points in the range (latitude) (Fig. 1-7). In other words, in order to be able to consider a curve continuous or discontinuous, we must first define a domain and range and then analyze the transformation to see whether points close to each other in the domain are mapped into points that are close to each other in the range.

The same is true in the illustration of the animal track. We are not considering points on the tail as being transferred from one place to another; we are discussing the transfer of points from our created domain into points of our created range.

The procedure used to find the point in the range that

Figure 1-7

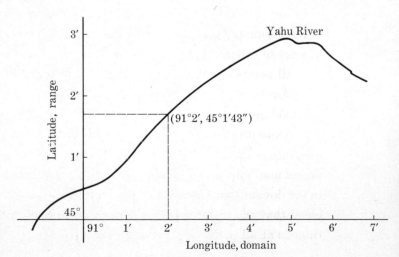

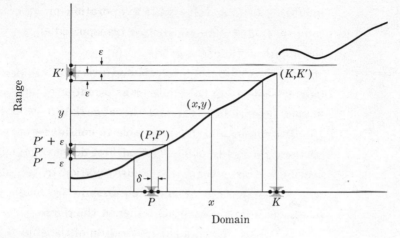

Figure 1-8

is the image of the point x in the domain is to draw a vertical line up from x until it hits the track at a point and then to draw a horizontal line from this point of intersection to the left until it intersects the range. The point y where the horizontal line intersects the range is called the *image* of the *preimage* x. The point on the track is denoted by the ordered pair (x, y). The track is thought of as consisting of a set of ordered pairs.

All points close to P in Fig. 1-8 map into points which are close to P', but all points close to K do not map into points close to K'. The animal lifted his tail at point (K, K'); consequently, points which are close to K on its left map into points close to K', but points close to K on its right do *not* map into points close to K'. Except at the point K in the domain, we can say that the track is continuous. We mean that the transformation induced by the track is continuous at all points in its domain except K.

Each little concave box (Fig. 1-8) in the domain and range is used to represent the set of points which are within a prescribed closeness to the point at its center. These concave boxes (open intervals) represent one-dimensional neighborhoods. A point in such a box is within a prescribed ε- or δ-distance from the point at its center.

If we draw a vertical line up from a point x close to K on the right in Fig. 1-9, we do not reach the track until we are much higher than the point (K, K'). Consequently, when we draw the horizontal line over to the range, it will intersect the range at a point outside *some* ε-neighborhood of K'. Unless, for *any* positive real number ε, we can find a δ-closeness to K so that all points within this δ-neighborhood of K will map into this preassigned ε-neighborhood of K', we shall say that the track is discontinuous at the point K.

In Fig. 1-8, any point within the δ-neighborhood of P maps into a point which is *closer* to P' than the point $P' + \varepsilon$

Figure 1-9

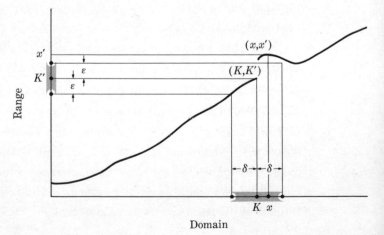

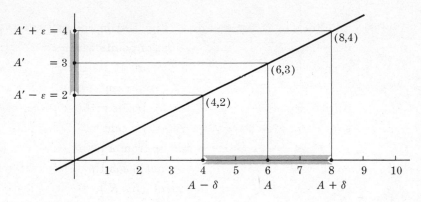

Figure 1-10

or the point $P' - \varepsilon$. We have agreed that this means that if we draw a vertical line up from any point in the δ-neighborhood of P until it touches the track and then draw a horizontal line to the range, the horizontal line will intersect the range at some point which is within the ε-neighborhood of P'.

The track is continuous at P if for every ε-neighborhood of P' we can find a δ-neighborhood of P with the property that any point in the δ-neighborhood is mapped to a point within the ε-neighborhood of P'.

Now that we have introduced the basic ideas behind continuity, we can take a closer look at several of the statements we have been discussing. The simple graph of Fig. 1-10 represents the set of ordered pairs (x, y) of real numbers where $y = \frac{1}{2}x$. It is a transformation in which an ε-closeness of one unit in the range would demand a δ-closeness of no more than two units in the domain. This is the same as saying that any point within a two-unit neighborhood of A will map into a point within a one-unit neighborhood of A'

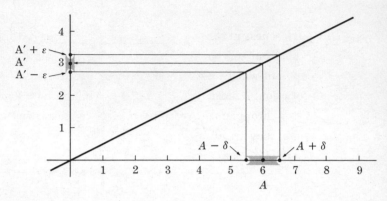

Figure 1-11

under the equation $y = \frac{1}{2}x$. However, if we are required to be within $\varepsilon = \frac{1}{4}$, we must choose $\delta \leq \frac{1}{2}$ to ensure that everything in the δ-neighborhood maps into the ε-neighborhood (Fig. 1-11).

Another continuous function is the set of ordered pairs (x, y) where $y = 2x$ (Fig. 1-12). We look upon this function as a transformation which maps points from the domain of the real numbers into the range of real numbers. For any

Figure 1-12

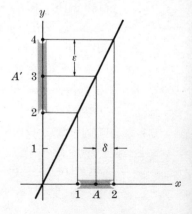

ε-closeness in the range, there is a δ-closeness in the domain such that any point which is δ-close to this point in the domain will be ε-close to its image in the range. For this function, δ must be no more than one-half as big as ε.

Throughout this study ε and δ are never negative numbers; they are always positive real numbers. Consequently, *ε and δ are never zero.*

Chapter Two: *Limit of a Sequence*

The following programmed exercises are a heuristic introduction to sequences. They constitute a get-your-feet-wet experience which will help you swim through the rest of the chapter.

The programmed exercises are divided into sections, called frames. Each frame has two main parts. The first part is called the stimulus and the second the response. They are separated by short horizontal bars. It is important that you use the following procedure on each frame:

1: Cover the response part of the frame with a card.

2: Write your response to the stimulus on a sheet of paper.

3: Compare your response with that of the author.

Of course one may attempt to save time by simply thinking the response instead of writing it. This is fine if one can be truthful with oneself, but it is too easy to read the author's response and say, "That is what I thought." If you write your own response, you can check the minute differences between your written response and the author's. These differences are often significant.

2-1: If we divide 1 by each of the natural numbers, i.e., by each of the positive integers, we have an infinite list of real numbers called a sequence: ($\frac{1}{1}$, $\frac{1}{2}$, $\frac{1}{3}$, $\frac{1}{4}$, . . .). Generate a sequence by dividing 2 by each of the natural numbers.

($\frac{2}{1}$, $\frac{2}{2}$, $\frac{2}{3}$, $\frac{2}{4}$, . . .). The three dots can be read "and so on."

2 - 2 : $\frac{1}{1}$ is the first term of the sequence ($\frac{1}{1}$, $\frac{1}{2}$, $\frac{1}{3}$, . . .), and $\frac{1}{9}$ is the ninth term. What are the first and ninth terms of the sequence you generated in 2-1?

$\frac{2}{1}$, $\frac{2}{9}$

2 - 3 : $1/n$ is the general term in the sequence ($\frac{1}{1}$, $\frac{1}{2}$, $\frac{1}{3}$, . . .). What is the general term in the sequence ($\frac{2}{1}$, $\frac{2}{2}$, $\frac{2}{3}$, . . .)?

$2/n$

2 - 4 : A sequence can be described by its general term. We can represent the sequence ($\frac{1}{1}$, $\frac{1}{2}$, $\frac{1}{3}$, . . .) by the symbolism $(1/n)$. How would you represent the sequence ($\frac{2}{1}$, $\frac{2}{2}$, $\frac{2}{3}$, . . .)?

$(2/n)$. The parentheses are used to indicate that this is a sequence, not just the general term.

2 - 5 : List the first three terms of the sequence $(3/n)$.

$\frac{3}{1}$, $\frac{3}{2}$, $\frac{3}{3}$

2 - 6 : List the first four terms of the sequence $(1/n^2)$.

$\frac{1}{1}$, $\frac{1}{4}$, $\frac{1}{9}$, $\frac{1}{16}$

2 - 7 : The sequence $(1, 8, 27, 64, \ldots)$ is represented by (n^3). The general term of this sequence is represented by n^3 without the parentheses. List the first four terms of the sequence $(n^3 + 1)$ and state its general term.

———

2, 9, 28, 65 are the first four terms. $(2, 9, 28, 65, \ldots, n^3 + 1, \ldots)$ is the sequence. $n^3 + 1$ is the general term.

———

2 - 8 : What is the general term of $(\frac{1}{2}, \frac{1}{4}, \frac{1}{8}, \frac{1}{16}, \ldots)$?

———

$1/2^n$ or $(\frac{1}{2})^n$

———

2 - 9 : Sequences can take many other forms. $(n^2/(n + 1))$ is the sequence _____.

———

$(\frac{1}{2}, \frac{4}{3}, \frac{9}{4}, \frac{16}{5}, \ldots)$

———

2 - 10 : In the sequence $(1/n)$ each successive term is smaller than the previous term. The 100th term is _____, and the 1,000th term is _____. The 1,000,001st term is _____ (greater, less) than the 1,000,000th term.

———

$\frac{1}{100}$, 1/1,000, less

———

2 - 11 : If we graph the sequence $(1/n)$, we notice that each neighborhood of 0 contains an infinite number of terms of the sequence. In fact each neighborhood of 0 contains *all but a finite number* of the terms of the sequence $(1/n)$.

If each neighborhood of a real number L contains *all but a finite number* of the terms of a sequence, then we say

All but a finite number of the terms of the sequence $(1/n)$ are within a distance of $1/10$ of 0.

All but a finite number of the terms of the sequence $(1 + 1/n)$ are within a distance of $1/10$ of 1.

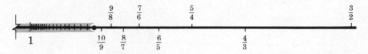

All but a finite number of the terms of the sequence $(2 + 1/n)$ are within a distance of $1/10$ of 2.

that L is the limit of the sequence. The limit of the sequence $(1 + 1/n)$ is 1 since each neighborhood of 1 contains all but a finite number of terms of the sequence $(1 + 1/n)$.

What is the limit of the sequence $(2 + 1/n)$?

2

2-12 : The distance between the seventh and eighth terms of the sequence $(1/n)$ is $\frac{1}{7} - \frac{1}{8} = \frac{1}{56}$. What is the difference between the limit and the millionth term?

$1/1,000,000 - 0 = 1/1,000,000$

2-13 : The terms of the sequence $(1/n)$ are successively closer to each other. $\frac{1}{4}$ is closer to $\frac{1}{8}$ than $\frac{1}{4}$ is to $\frac{1}{2}$ because $\frac{1}{4} - \frac{1}{8} = \frac{1}{8}$ is less than $\frac{1}{2} - \frac{1}{4} = \frac{1}{4}$. What is the largest distance between two consecutive terms of the sequence $(1/n)$?

___

½

___

2 - 14 : If we let $N = 1,000,000$, we can say that for all natural numbers n greater than N the terms of the sequence $(1/n)$ are _____ 0 than $1/N$.

(closer to, farther from)

___

Closer to

___

2 - 15 : There are a(n) _____ number of terms of $(1/n)$ which

(infinite, finite)

are within a distance of 0.2 of 0.   What is the largest term of the sequence which is closer to the limit than 0.2?

Infinite, ⅙

___

2 - 16 : If $n \geq N$, what value must N assume to assure that all terms of the sequence $(1/n)$ will be closer to 0 than 0.3?

___

$N \geq 4$, since $\frac{1}{4} = {}^{15}\!/_{60} < {}^{18}\!/_{60} = {}^{3}\!/_{10}$.

___

2 - 17 : No matter how small a number is chosen, it is always possible to find a term of the sequence $(1/n)$ that is closer to 0 than that number.   All terms beyond this term are also _____ than the chosen number.

___

Closer to 0

___

2 - 1 8 : The value of $1/n$ is never actually equal to 0, no matter how large n is. However, we can make $1/n$ as close as we please to 0, by choosing _____ values for n.

(larger, smaller)

————

Larger

————

In the first chapter we talked intuitively about animal tracks, transformations, mappings, graphs of rivers, and graphs of equations. Now we discuss similar abstract correspondences called *functions*. The transformation or mapping which we derived from the animal track was a function. The graph of the equation $y = 2x$ we shall now call a function.

A function is a correspondence which pairs elements of a set D, the domain of the function, with elements of a set R, the range of the function. We can describe the function $f:D \rightarrow R$ by listing all the ordered pairs (d, r) of the correspondence. The correspondence which matches every element in the domain $\{1, 2, 3\}$ with twice that element in the range $\{2, 4, 6\}$ may be represented by the set of ordered pairs $f = \{(1, 2), (2, 4), (3, 6)\}$. This same function can be described as $f = \{(x, y)|y = 2x, x \in \{1, 2, 3\}\}$. This symbolism is read "f is equal to the set of all ordered pairs (x, y) such that y is equal to $2x$ and x is an element of the domain $\{1, 2, 3\}$."

A function is a one-way pairing process. We think of the function f as carrying 1 to 2, 2 to 4, and 3 to 6, but not vice versa, as the arrows indicate in Fig. 2-1. We think of each ordered pair as mapping the first element onto the second element, so that the ordered pair (d, r) differs from

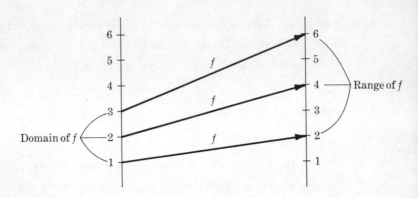

Figure 2-1

the ordered pair (r, d), the first element in (d, r) being d, whereas the first element in (r, d) is r.

We further restrict a function so that the first element is not allowed to map onto two different second elements, but we shall allow several of the first elements to be mapped onto a common second element.

DEFINITION 2-1:

A function is a set of ordered pairs no two of which have the same first element. The *domain* of the function is the set of first elements of the ordered pairs, and the *range* is the set of second elements of the ordered pairs.

If f is a function, we shall indicate that f maps d onto r by writing

$$f(d) = r$$

which means that the ordered pair (d, r) is an element of f

$$(d, r) \in f$$

When we write $f(d) = r$, we are asserting that r is the *value* of the function at d. When we write $f(x) = x^2 + 3x$, we mean that $x^2 + 3x$ is the value of the function f at the point x in the domain of the function

$$f = \{(x, y)|y = x^2 + 3x, x \in \text{Re}\}$$

which is sometimes written

$$f = \{(x, x^2 + 3x)\}$$

The graph of the equation $y = 2x$ is the set of ordered pairs of the form $(a, 2a)$, where a is a real number. We shall often write this function as $\{(x, y)|y = 2x, x \in \text{Re}\}$. This symbolism is read "the set of all ordered pairs (x, y) such that y is equal to $2x$ and x is an element of the set of real numbers."

2-19 : The set of ordered pairs $\{(1, 3), (3, 7), (4, 9), (2, 5)\}$ is a function. For every element in the domain there is one and only one element in the range. The domain of the function is the set $\{1, 3, 4, 2\}$, and the range is the set $\{3, 7, 9, 5\}$. Is the set of ordered pairs $\{(1, 2), (3, 6), (4, 8), (2, 4)\}$ a function? What is its domain? What is its range?

———

Yes, it is a function. $\{1, 2, 3, 4\}$ is the domain, and $\{2, 4, 6, 8\}$ is the range.

———

2-20 : Definition 2-1 describes a function as a set of ordered pairs in which no two ordered pairs have the same first element. $\{(1, 3), (2, 4), (1, 5), (3, 6)\}$ is not a function since $(1, 3)$ and $(1, 5)$ both have the same first element.

Is $\{(2, 4), (2, 3), (3, 5), (4, 2)\}$ a function?

No; $(2, 4)$ and $(2, 3)$ both have the same first element.

2 - 21 : We often describe a function by stating its domain and range and then describing the ordered pairs by an equation which gives the image y of any point x in the domain.

Example: The function in 2-19 is a function from the domain $\{1, 2, 3, 4\}$ onto the range $\{2, 4, 6, 8\}$. This fact may be symbolized $f:\{1, 2, 3, 4\} \rightarrow \{2, 4, 6, 8\}$. A complete description of the function is

$$f = \{(x, y)|y = 2x, x \in \{1, 2, 3, 4\}\}$$

Consider the function from the real numbers onto the real numbers, $f:\text{Re} \rightarrow \text{Re}$, described by the equation $y = 3x - 2$. What are the domain, range, graph, and description of this function? Use Re to denote the set of real numbers.

The domain and range are both the set of real numbers. We shall graph the domain on the x axis and the range on the y axis. The function itself is the infinite set of points that make up the graphed line $y = 3x - 2$. $f = \{(x, y)|y = 3x - 2, x \in \text{Re}\}$.

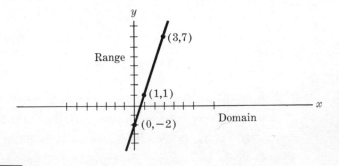

2 - 2 2 : Is the following set of ordered pairs a function: $\{(2, 3), (3, 4),$ $(5, 6), (1, 1)\}$? What is the domain? What is the range?

————

Yes, it is a function. The domain is $\{1, 2, 3, 5\}$, and the range is $\{1, 3, 4, 6\}$.

————

DEFINITION 2-2:

A sequence is a function whose domain is a subset of the natural numbers.

In this book a sequence is a set of ordered pairs, for example, $\{(1, f_1), (2, f_2), (3, f_3), (4, f_4), \ldots, (n, f_n)\}$, in which the first coordinate in each ordered pair is a natural number and the second coordinate is a real number. The set of first coordinates is the *domain* of the sequence, and the set of second coordinates is the *range* of the sequence. Since the ordering of the natural numbers is so well known, it is customary to shorten this notation to an ordered set of range elements, which we symbolize $(f_1, f_2, f_3, f_4, \ldots, f_n)$.

Example: The first five natural numbers divisible by 3 are the range elements of a function defined on the domain $\{1, 2, 3, 4, 5\}$ whose range is the set $\{3, 6, 9, 12, 15\}$. This function is the *finite* sequence $\{(1, 3), (2, 6), (3, 9), (4, 12), (5, 15)\}$. It is shortened to $(3, 6, 9, 12, 15)$.

Example: All positive integers divisible by 2 are the range elements of the *infinite* sequence $\{(1, 2), (2, 4), (3, 6), \ldots, (n, 2n), \ldots\}$, which is shortened to $(2, 4, 6, \ldots, 2n, \ldots)$ or to $(2n)$.

Notice that when we indicate a finite sequence, we place the general term last: $(f_1, f_2, f_3, \ldots, f_n)$; but when we want to indicate an infinite sequence, we add three dots beyond the general term $(f_1, f_2, f_3, \ldots, f_n, \ldots)$ or write (f_n). If the form of the general term is obvious, we may write simply $(f_1, f_2, f_3, \ldots)$ for an infinite sequence.

Suppose a frog at the bottom of a well finds himself cast under a spell which allows him to jump half the distance out of the well on its first attempt and half the remaining distance on each successive jump (Fig. 2-2). Will the frog ever free himself from the well? The successive distances that the frog jumps form a *distance sequence* $(\frac{1}{2}, \frac{1}{4}, \frac{1}{8}, \ldots, 1/2^n, \ldots)$. If it takes the frog 1 second between jumps and $1/2^n$ second to travel the nth distance, then the times it takes for the halvings of the distances out of the well form a *time sequence* $(\frac{3}{2}, \frac{5}{4}, \frac{9}{8}, \ldots, 1 + 1/2^n, \ldots)$.

Even though the terms of the distance sequence become very small, almost everyone agrees that the frog will never

Figure 2-2

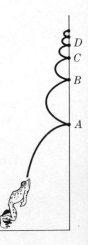

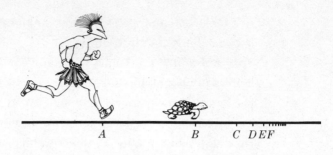

Figure 2-3

free himself. Before discussing this conclusion, however, consider the following problem. It is quite similar, but the usual answer seems to contradict the answer we have just obtained.

The philosopher Zeno, who lived in Elea, on the shore of southern Italy, around 500 B.C., formulated the following paradox, in which his reasoning seems to indicate that Achilles cannot catch a tortoise if he allows the tortoise a handicap. Achilles starts at A (Fig. 2-3) and the tortoise at B. It will take Achilles a time T_1 to run the distance to B. In this same amount of time, the tortoise has moved to C. So Achilles has a distance to travel before he overtakes the tortoise. It will take him time T_2 to cover the remaining distance to C, but during this time the tortoise has moved to D. Achilles still has to cover the distance the tortoise walked during his last time interval. He will require a time T_3 to run this distance, but the tortoise will make some more progress during T_3. This leaves Achilles with a fourth distance to run; and, of course, the tortoise will make some more progress during T_4. Zeno asks whether this will continue forever, as Achilles will always have some small distance to run. While he is running this distance, the tortoise will make some progress, leaving Achilles another distance between himself and the tortoise.

If A and B are 1 mile apart and Achilles is running at 2 miles per hour while the tortoise is crawling at only 1 mile per hour, then experience has shown that Achilles will pass the tortoise in precisely 1 hour. This then is the paradox: How can Achilles take an infinite number of halvings of the distance between himself and the tortoise in a finite amount of time?

Study the following table and see whether you can give an answer to Zeno's paradox before reading on.

Total time	Achilles' position	Tortoise's position	Distance between Achilles and tortoise
0	$0 = A$	$1 = B$	1
$\frac{1}{2}$	$1 = B$	$\frac{3}{2} = C$	$\frac{1}{2}$
$\frac{3}{4}$	$\frac{3}{2} = C$	$\frac{7}{4} = D$	$\frac{1}{4}$
$\frac{7}{8}$	$\frac{7}{4} = D$	$1\frac{5}{8} = E$	$\frac{1}{8}$
$1\frac{5}{16}$	$1\frac{5}{8} = E$	$3\frac{1}{16} = F$	$\frac{1}{16}$
$3\frac{1}{32}$	$3\frac{1}{16} = F$	$6\frac{3}{32} = G$	$\frac{1}{32}$
$6\frac{3}{64}$	$6\frac{3}{32} = G$	$12\frac{7}{64} = H$	$\frac{1}{64}$

So after the sixth halving Achilles still has $\frac{1}{64}$ mile to cover before overtaking the tortoise. After 1 million of such halvings will Achilles have passed the tortoise? The distances between the two, starting from the time Achilles is at B, form the sequence $(\frac{1}{2}, \frac{1}{4}, \frac{1}{8}, \ldots, 1/2^n, \ldots)$. The times it takes for these halvings form the time sequence $(\frac{1}{2}, \frac{1}{4}, \frac{1}{8}, \ldots, 1/2^n, \ldots)$. The terms of both of these sequences become progressively smaller, but are any of the terms actually zero?

Comparing Achilles' problem and the frog's problem, one sees that they are very similar. In time T_1 Achilles halves the distance to the tortoise. He halves the remaining distance in each successive time interval just as the frog does, yet we intuitively feel that Achilles does catch the tortoise and the frog never escapes from the well. Is there something different about the two problems which will allow Achilles to catch the tortoise yet prohibit the frog from leaving the well?

Their time sequences are different. Achilles will take a total time of $\frac{1}{2} + \frac{1}{4} + \frac{1}{8} + \cdots + 1/2^n + \cdots$ to catch the tortoise, whereas the frog's total time in jumping out of the well is $\frac{3}{2} + \frac{5}{4} + \frac{9}{8} + \cdots + (1 + 1/2^n) + \cdots$. We shall refer to this type of sum as the *sum of a time sequence* or *time series*. It will take several pages to explain the difference between these two sums, but in a nutshell we shall show that the sum of Achilles' time sequence is 1, which indicates that he will have taken an infinite number of halvings in 1 hour; whereas the sum of the frog's time sequence increases without bound, indicating that the frog will not have the time to make an infinite number of halvings.

In other words, if the frog did not take the extra second after each jump, he would reach the top of the well; and if the tortoise and Achilles took a second's rest after each halving, Achilles would not catch the tortoise.

The resolution of the paradox depends upon the demonstration that Achilles can take an infinite number of halvings in a finite amount of time, so we interrupt the discussion to show that the sum of the time sequence $(\frac{1}{2}, \frac{1}{4}, \frac{1}{8}, \ldots)$ is 1. We show later that $a_1/(1 - r)$ is the sum of a geometric progression $a_1 + ra_1 + r^2a_1 + \cdots + r^{n-1}a_1 + \cdots$, where $|r| < 1$. If we investigate the sum of the time sequence $(\frac{1}{2}, \frac{1}{4}, \frac{1}{8}, \ldots)$, we see that the ratio r between terms is $\frac{1}{2}$ and the first term a_1 is also $\frac{1}{2}$. The sum $\frac{1}{2} + \frac{1}{4} + \frac{1}{8} + \cdots + 1/2^n + \cdots$ is thus

$$\frac{\frac{1}{2}}{(1 - \frac{1}{2})} = 1$$

This formula for the sum of a geometric progression therefore indicates that Achilles has closed the mile between himself and the tortoise in 1 hour, since the sums of both the time and distance sequences are 1.

Will the frog ever reach the top of the well? He jumps $(\frac{1}{2}, \frac{1}{4}, \ldots, 1/2^n, \ldots)$, which is a geometric progression of distances whose sum is 1, but the frog's time series, $\frac{3}{2} + \frac{5}{4} + \frac{9}{8} + \cdots + (1 + 1/2^n) + \cdots$, does not have any real number for its value. Here is where the praradox really lies. Can Achilles really *walk past* an infinite number of points? Yes, it is done every day. Can the frog jump an *infinite* number of times? Not if it takes at least a second for each jump. If the frog could take an infinite number of jumps in his finite lifetime, he would reach the top. The frog cannot take an infinite number of jumps because each jump will use up at least a second, and his lifetime is not long enough to allow an infinite number of seconds. On the other hand, Achilles can walk past an infinite number of points if we do not insist that he stop momentarily at each point.

In effect, Zeno is asking, "Can Achilles take an infinite

number of halvings of the distance between himself and the tortoise if each of the halvings takes a second?" We must admit that if each halving takes at least a second, Achilles can never catch the tortoise. One can argue that Zeno certainly realized that some of the halvings would take less than 1 second. Actually, Zeno had in mind a chronon (the smallest possible bit of time). In this smallest piece of time, Achilles could make at most a single halving, then in the next chronon a single halving, and on and on ad infinitum.

Since it has been demonstrated that if Achilles travels at 2 miles per hour for 1 hour, he will accomplish an infinite number of halvings in the last second, it appears that there is no such thing as a chronon; i.e., time is not quantized.

Figure 2-4 illustrates another example, which shows the difference between walking past an infinite number of points and stopping for an instant of time at each point. In this problem each of four robot mice is placed in the corner of a square room and is programmed to follow his neighbor to

Figure 2-4

the right. When a switch is thrown, each moves toward his neighbor and will continue to follow him regardless of where he goes.

The robots will circle the point in the center of the room an infinite number of times. Assuming that they are small enough to fit into one point, will they ever reach the center of the room? If they make 10 revolutions per second, they will never reach the center, because there are not an infinite number of seconds available. If they are traveling at 10 feet per second, they can complete an infinite number of revolutions in the last second, and since the length of the spiral they travel is finite, they will reach the center.

In the foregoing discussion we assumed that the sum of a geometric progression is given by $a_1/(1 - r)$, where $|r| < 1$. We now show that the assumption was correct. The expression $a_1/(1 - r)$ is usually derived from the formula $s_n = (a_1 - a_1 r^n)/(1 - r)$, which is the formula for the sum of the first n terms of a geometric progression, and which we now derive.

Let s_n be the sum of the first n terms of the geometric progression. Then we may write

$$s_n = a_1 + a_1 r + a_1 r^2 + \cdots + a_1 r^{n-1}$$

If we multiply by r, we obtain

$$r s_n = a_1 r + a_1 r^2 + a_1 r^3 + \cdots + a_1 r^{n-1} + a_1 r^n$$

Subtracting $r s_n$ from s_n, we see that all terms cancel except a_1 and $a_1 r^n$,

$$s_n - r s_n = a_1 - a_1 r^n$$
$$s_n(1 - r) = a_1 - a_1 r^n$$
$$s_n = \frac{a_1 - a_1 r^n}{1 - r}$$

The next step in the derivation rests on the important concept of limit, a difficult concept that will take the rest of the book to explain completely. It is argued that if r is a number between zero and one, then r^n approaches zero as n increases without bound. Hence, the sum of an infinite number of terms is

$$\frac{a_1 - (a_1)(0)}{1 - r} = \frac{a_1}{1 - r}$$

We symbolize this fact

$$\lim_{n \to \infty} \frac{a_1 - a_1 r^n}{1 - r} = \frac{a_1}{1 - r} \qquad \text{if } 0 < r < 1$$

To investigate this fact further we need to define precisely what we mean when we say "the limit of the sequence $(1/2^n)$ as n increases without bound is 0." We symbolize this statement

$$\lim_{n \to \infty} \frac{1}{2^n} = 0$$

The symbolism $\lim\limits_{n \to \infty} 1/2^n = 0$ is defined to mean

for each positive real number ε
there exists a natural number N
    such that
if n is greater than or equal to N, then the positive difference between $1/2^n$ and 0 is less than ε.

This may be symbolized

$$n \geq N \Rightarrow \left| \frac{1}{2^n} - 0 \right| < \varepsilon$$

This definition is in essence the same as the definition in frame 2-11. There we state that 0 is the limit of the sequence $(1/2^n)$ if all but a finite number of terms of the sequence are in each neighborhood of 0. In the ε-definition we insist that all but a finite number of the terms of the sequence be within each ε-neighborhood of 0. The finite number of terms that come before the Nth term might be outside the ε-neighborhood of 0. The Nth term and the infinite number of terms which lie beyond it (the nth terms where $n \geq N$) are all within the ε-neighborhood.

To explain this definition we inject another example. Suppose Achilles decides to walk from town A to town B, a distance of 1 mile (Fig. 2-5). He will walk $\frac{1}{2}$ mile $+$ $\frac{1}{4}$ mile $+$ $\frac{1}{8}$ mile $+$ $\cdots$ until he has covered the distance between the towns. This definition amounts to a contest between Achilles and a mysterious person called Epsilon. Epsilon stands as close as he pleases to town B, but Achilles can be closer to town by walking past the Nth halving (Fig. 2-6).

If Epsilon is standing $\frac{1}{10}$ mile from town B, then Achilles, after walking past the fourth halving, is closer to town than Epsilon. Every halving after the fourth will find Achilles even closer to town. This can be shortened to

Figure 2-5

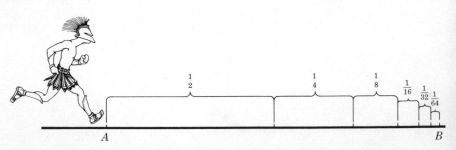

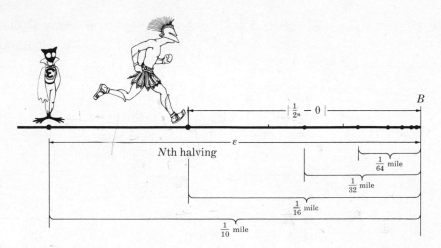

Figure 2-6

$n \geq 4 \Rightarrow |1/2^n - 0| < \frac{1}{10}$, i.e., if n is greater than or equal to 4, then the distance between $1/2^n$ and 0 is less than $\frac{1}{10}$.

Suppose Epsilon is 0.01 mile from town; then Achilles is closer to town than Epsilon after the seventh halving. That is, $n \geq 7$ will make $|1/2^n - 0| < 0.01$.

The limit of the sequence $(1/2^n)$ is 0 as n becomes infinite if Achilles can always come closer to town than Epsilon. Because there are always an infinite number of halvings closer to 0 than any closeness Epsilon can find, all but a finite number of halvings will be closer than Epsilon.

The following programmed exercise is designed to give a more thorough understanding of these ideas.

2-23 : If $\lim 1/2^n = 0$, then

for each positive real number ε
there exists a natural number N

such that

$$n \geq N \Rightarrow \left| \frac{1}{2^n} - 0 \right| < \varepsilon$$

Statements that have the above form can be thought of as describing a game. Mr. Epsilon is the challenger, and the reader is the defender. The challenger assigns values to the symbols which follow "for each," and the defender assigns values to all symbols that follow "there exists." If the challenger assigns a value of 0.1 for ε, we shall have to specify an N of 4 so that $n \geq 4 \Rightarrow |1/2^n - 0| < 0.1$. If we are challenged by an ε of 0.01, what is the smallest value of N which will assure that $n \geq N \Rightarrow |1/2^n - 0| < 0.01$?

―――――――

$N = 7$; since $|1/2^7 - 0| = \frac{1}{128}$, which is less than 0.01.

―――――――

2-24 : If we are given the challenge to find an N so that $n \geq N \Rightarrow |1/2^n - 0| < \frac{1}{50}$, we can choose an $N = 6$ since

$|1/2^6 - 0| = \frac{1}{64} < \frac{1}{50}$

Find an N so that $n \geq N \Rightarrow |1/2^n - 0| < \frac{1}{200}$.

―――――――

$N \geq 8$. Any natural number greater than 8 will work.

―――――――

2-25 : What N could you choose so that $n \geq N \Rightarrow |1/2^n - 0| < 1/1,000,000$? *Hint:* $2^{20} = 1,048,576$; $2^{19} = 524,288$.

―――――――

$N \geq 20$. 20 is the smallest N that will satisfy the statement, but any larger N will also satisfy it.

―――――――

2-26 : The definition of $\lim\limits_{n \to \infty} 1/2^n = 0$ is

for each positive real number ε

there exists a natural number N

such that

$$n \geq N \Rightarrow \left| \frac{1}{2^n} - 0 \right| < \varepsilon$$

Define $\lim\limits_{n \to \infty} 1/n = 0.$

———

The definition of $\lim\limits_{n \to \infty} 1/n = 0$ is

for each positive real number ε
there exists a natural number N
   such that

$$n \geq N \Rightarrow \left| \frac{1}{n} - 0 \right| < \varepsilon$$

———

2-27 : The sequence $(1/n)$ is $(1/1, 1/2, 1/3, \ldots, 1/n, \ldots)$. If we are given $\varepsilon = 1/8$, we wish to find an N so that $|1/n - 0| < 1/8$ for $n \geq N$. If we choose $N = 9$, then for any number n greater than or equal to 9, $|1/n - 0| < 1/8$. We are saying that the ninth term and all the following terms are closer to 0 than $1/8$. Find an N so that $n \geq N \Rightarrow |1/n - 0| < 0.01$.

———

$N \geq 101$

———

2-28 : What N could you choose so that $n \geq N \Rightarrow |1/n - 0| < 0.001$?

———

$N \geq 1,001$

———

2-29 : What is the definition of $\lim\limits_{n \to \infty} \dfrac{n^2 + 1}{n^2 - 1} = 1$? Be sure that you indicate that the terms of the sequence are approaching 1, that is, $|(n^2 + 1)/(n^2 - 1) - 1|$ is small for sufficiently large n.

———

$$\lim_{n \to \infty} \frac{n^2 + 1}{n^2 - 1} = 1 \text{ is defined to mean that}$$

for each positive real number ε
there exists a natural number N
such that

$$n \geq N \Rightarrow \left| \frac{n^2 + 1}{n^2 - 1} - 1 \right| < \varepsilon$$

———

2-30 : $\lim\limits_{n \to \infty} \dfrac{3n^2 - 1}{n^2 - 1} = 3$ is defined to mean that _____.

———

For each positive real number ε
there exists a natural number N
such that

$$n \geq N \Rightarrow \left| \frac{3n^2 - 1}{n^2 - 1} - 3 \right| < \varepsilon$$

The following figure is a graph of several of the members of the sequence. Notice how they bunch up near the limit of the sequence. One might say that every neighborhood of 3 contains an infinite number of points of the sequence. Each neighborhood contains all but a finite number of terms.

———

2-31 : $\lim\limits_{n \to \infty} \dfrac{n^2 - 1}{1 - n^2} = -1$ is defined

for each positive real number ε
there exists a natural number N

such that

___

$$n \geq N \Rightarrow \left| \frac{n^2 - 1}{1 - n^2} - (-1) \right| < \varepsilon$$

___

2-32: List the elements of the sequence $|(n^2 - 1)/(1 - n^2)|$. Since this sequence is not defined for $n = 1$, it will be necessary to consider the sequence as having a domain consisting of the natural numbers larger than 1.

___

$-1, -1, -1, \ldots$

___

2-33: $\lim\limits_{n - \infty} 1/3^n = 0$ is defined to mean _____.

> For each real number $\varepsilon > 0$
> there exists an $N > 0$
>> such that
>> $$n \geq N \Rightarrow \left| \frac{1}{3^n} - 0 \right| < \varepsilon$$

___

2-34: List the elements of the sequence $(-\tfrac{1}{2})^n$.

___

$-\tfrac{1}{2}, \tfrac{1}{4}, -\tfrac{1}{8}, \tfrac{1}{16}, \ldots, (-\tfrac{1}{2})^n, \ldots$

2-35: Graph the first six terms of $(-\tfrac{1}{2})^n$ on the following number line:

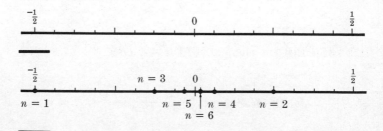

___

2-36: The infinite sequence $2 - (-\frac{1}{2})^n$ has the limit 2. When this sequence is graphed, the range elements of the sequence are alternately greater and smaller than 2, but each term is closer to 2 than the previous term. In any neighborhood of 2 there are an infinite number of terms of the sequence, and each neighborhood contains all but a finite number of terms of the sequence. List the elements of the sequence $(2 - (-\frac{1}{2})^n)$.

$\frac{5}{2}, \frac{7}{4}, 1\frac{7}{8}, 3\frac{1}{16}, \ldots, \dfrac{2^{(n+1)} - (-1)^n}{2^n}, \ldots$

Notice: $\dfrac{2^{(n+1)} - (-1)^n}{2^n} = 2 - (-\frac{1}{2})^n$

2-37: $\lim\limits_{n \to \infty} (2 - (-\frac{1}{2})^n) = 2$ is defined:

for each positive real number ϵ
there exists a natural number N
such that

_____.

$n \geq N \Rightarrow |(2 - (-\frac{1}{2})^n) - 2| < \epsilon$

2-38: List the elements of the sequence $(2 + (-\frac{1}{2})^n)$.

$\frac{3}{2}, \frac{9}{4}, 1\frac{5}{8}, 3\frac{3}{16}, \ldots, \dfrac{2^{(n+1)} + (-1)^n}{2^n}, \ldots$

2-39: Graph the first six terms of $2 + (-\frac{1}{2})^n$ on the following number line:

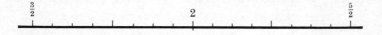

The graph is like that in 2-35 except that the center point is at 2.

2-40: What is $\lim\limits_{n \to \infty} (2 + (-\frac{1}{2})^n)$?

$$\lim_{n \to \infty} (2 + (-\tfrac{1}{2})^n) = 2$$

2-41: List the elements of the sequence $(3 - (\frac{1}{2})^n)$.

$$\tfrac{5}{2}, \, 1\tfrac{1}{4}, \, 2\tfrac{3}{8}, \, 4\tfrac{7}{16}, \, 9\tfrac{5}{32}, \ldots, \frac{3(2)^n - 1}{2^n}, \ldots$$

The general term can be written in different forms:

$$3 - (\tfrac{1}{2})^n = 3 - \frac{1}{2^n} = \frac{3(2^n)}{2^n} - \frac{1}{2^n} = \frac{3(2^n) - 1}{2^n}$$

2-42: What is the limit of $(3 - (\frac{1}{2})^n)$ as n increases without bound?

$$3$$

2-43: What is the definition of $\lim\limits_{n \to \infty} (3 - (\frac{1}{2})^n) = 3$?

$\lim\limits_{n \to \infty} (3 - (\frac{1}{2})^n) = 3$ is defined to mean:

    for each positive real number ε
    there exists a natural number N
        such that
      $n \geq N \Rightarrow |(3 - (\tfrac{1}{2})^n) - 3| < \varepsilon$

2 - 4 4 : What is the smallest value that we could assign to N to assure that all the terms of $(3 - (\frac{1}{2})^n)$ beyond the Nth will be closer to 3 than 3.001? *Hint:* $2^{10} = 1{,}024$, and $2^9 = 512$.

———

$N = 10$.   Since, $n \geq 10 \Rightarrow |(3 - (\frac{1}{2})^n - 3| < 0.001$.

———

2 - 4 5 : Define the statement, "L is the limit of the infinite sequence (f_n) as n increases without bound."

DEFINITION 2 - 3 :

The symbolism $\lim\limits_{n \to \infty} f_n = L$ is defined to mean

for each positive real number ε
there exists a natural number N
   such that

$n \geq N \Rightarrow |f_n - L| < \varepsilon$

Chapter Three: Continuity

In Chap. 1 we showed that in the study of continuity, we are interested in whether a function graphs points which are close to each other in the domain into points which are close to each other in the range. We say that a function is continuous at a point c in its domain if and only if

> for each ε-neighborhood of $f(c)$
> there exists a δ-neighborhood of c
>   such that
> for each point x in the domain of f
> if x is in a δ-neighborhood of c, then $f(x)$ is in an ε-neighborhood of $f(c)$.

Figure 3-1 illustrates this definition, which suggests the same game of challenger and defender we played in Chap. 2. The challenger demands an ε-closeness to $f(c)$, and the defender answers with a δ such that all points of the domain of f which are in a δ-neighborhood of c will map into the given ε-neighborhood of $f(c)$. If a δ can be found, the defender wins, and the function is continuous at c.

We use the term *neighborhood* for a set which is also called an open interval, open sphere, open disc, or open ball. We like the term neighborhood, since it carries with it the

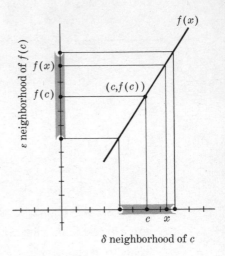

Figure 3-1

intuitive concept of nearness. When a person lives close to us, we say that he lives in our neighborhood. If x is a point whose distance from b is less than δ, we shall say that x is in a δ-neighborhood of b. If the distance from x to b

Figure 3-2

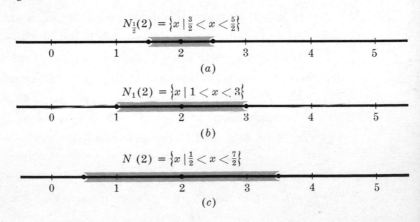

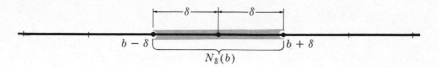

Figure 3-3

is less than 2, we shall say that x is within a neighborhood of radius 2 about b and symbolize it $x \in N_2(b)$.

In Fig. 3-2 we show a set of neighborhoods about the point 2 which are open intervals on the real line. The first neighborhood of 2 (Fig. 3-2a) has a radius of $\frac{1}{2}$ and consists of all the real numbers between $\frac{3}{2}$ and $\frac{5}{2}$. This sentence is symbolized $N_{\frac{1}{2}}(2) = \{x | \frac{3}{2} < x < \frac{5}{2}\}$, which is read "the neighborhood of radius $\frac{1}{2}$ about the point 2 is the set of all points x such that x is greater than $\frac{3}{2}$ and less than $\frac{5}{2}$." If x is in $N_{\frac{1}{2}}(2)$, then $|x - 2| < \frac{1}{2}$.

In Fig. 3-2b, the neighborhood $N_1(2)$ is the set $\{x | 1 < x < 3\}$, that is, the set of all x such that x is between 1 and 3. If x is in $N_1(2)$, then $|x - 2| < 1$.

In Fig. 3-2c, the neighborhood $N_{\frac{3}{2}}(2)$ is the set $\{x | \frac{1}{2} < x < \frac{7}{2}\}$. $x \in N_{\frac{3}{2}}(2) \Rightarrow |x - 2| < \frac{3}{2}$.

On the real line $N_\delta(b)$ is the neighborhood of radius δ about the point b (Fig. 3-3). The shaded part of the real line between $b - \delta$ and $b + \delta$ is the neighborhood of radius δ about b. The points $b - \delta$ and $b + \delta$ are not members of $N_\delta(b)$. $N_\delta(b) = \{x | b - \delta < x < b + \delta\}$.

3-1 : Graph $N_{\frac{3}{4}}(3)$.

3 - 2 : Graph $N_2(2)$

3 - 3 : Put this graphed neighborhood in short notation:

$N_\delta(3)$

3 - 4 : Put this neighborhood in short notation:

$N_2(3)$

3 - 5 : Put this neighborhood in short notation:

$N_\varepsilon(f(a))$

3 - 6 : A function is continuous at a point c in its domain if and only if

for each ε-neighborhood of $f(c)$

there exists a δ-neighborhood of c

such that

for each point x in the domain of f
if x is in a δ-neighborhood of c, then $f(x)$ is in an ε-neighborhood of $f(c)$.

Symbolize the italicized statement.

$$x \in N_{\delta}(c) \Rightarrow f(x) \in N_{\varepsilon}(f(c))$$

3-7 : Rewrite the definition for "f is continuous at a point b in the domain of f" using absolute-value signs to indicate distance. Observe that $|x - b| < \delta$ is equivalent to $x \in N_{\delta}(b)$. Similarly, $|f(x) - f(b)| < \varepsilon$ is equivalent to $f(x) \in N_{\varepsilon}(f(b))$.

DEFINITION 3-1:

A function f is continuous at a point b in the domain of f if and only if

    for each positive real number ε
    there exists a positive real number δ
        such that
    for each x in the domain of f

$$|x - b| < \delta \Rightarrow |f(x) - f(b)| < \varepsilon$$

This will be our definition of continuity at a point in the domain of a function.

Visualize a drumhead made of an elastic material that will withstand drastic deformations without tearing. This is a two-dimensional disc, upon which we may induce continuous transformations by straining or stretching. If we draw a curve on the head of the drum and then deform the

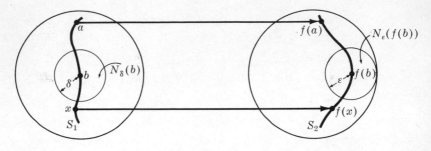

Figure 3-4

drawing by stretching it, the transformation induced is continuous.

Figure 3-4 illustrates a transformation induced by stretching the drumhead to the right. The curve S_1 is the domain of the transformation, and the curve S_2 is the range of the transformation. In transformations induced in this manner on our disc, for any neighborhood of $f(b)$ in the range there exists a neighborhood of b in the domain such that every point in the domain which is close to b is mapped into the given neighborhood of $f(b)$. In the above transformation, the point $f(b)$ is the image of the point b, and every point in the neighborhood $N_\delta(b)$ maps onto some point

Figure 3-5

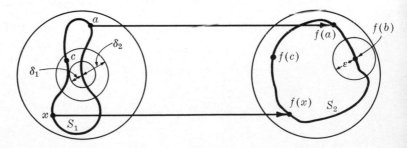

ε-close to $f(b)$. A point x is within $N_\delta(b)$ if the distance between x and b is less than δ.

In the following transformation pictured on the drumhead (Fig. 3-5), it is not true that every point of the domain within a δ_2-distance of b maps into $N_\varepsilon(f(b))$. That is, there is a point c of the domain which is δ_2-close to b that does *not* map into a point which is ε-close to $f(b)$ in the range.

However, there is a δ_1 such that every point of the domain which is δ_1-close to b is mapped into a point which is ε-close to $f(b)$. This can be symbolized $x \in N_{\delta_1}(b) \Rightarrow f(x) \in N_\varepsilon(f(b))$), which simply means that if the distance between x and b is less than δ_1, then the distance between $f(x)$ and $f(b)$ is less than ε. Since it is possible to find some δ-neighborhood of b for every ε-neighborhood of $f(b)$, we know that the function is continuous at b.

3 - 8 : Let f:Re $\to$ Re be the function $\{(x, y)|y = 3x + 1, x \in \text{Re}\}$. Suppose that we have been challenged to find a δ that will satisfy the statement

$$|x - 2| \leqslant \delta \Rightarrow |(3x + 1) - 7| < \tfrac{1}{2}$$

If f is continuous at the point 2, then such a δ exists. To find an exact value for δ, we shall start with the consequent, $|(3x + 1) - 7| < \tfrac{1}{2}$, and substitute different expressions on the left-hand side until we obtain something similar to the antecedent, $|x - 2| < \delta$. We shall call this process an exploration, for reasons which we shall explain later.

A : $|(3x + 1) - 7| < \tfrac{1}{2}$
B : $|3x - 6| < \tfrac{1}{2}$
C : $3|x - 2| < \tfrac{1}{2}$
D : $|x - 2| < \tfrac{1}{6}$

Now if we choose $\delta = \frac{1}{6}$, statement D is the same as the antecedent $|x - 2| < \delta$. So we can now prove that if $x \in N_{\frac{1}{6}}(2)$, then $f(x) \in N_{\frac{1}{2}}(7)$.

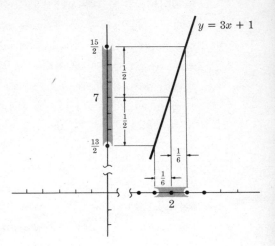

Proof:

1: $|x - 2| < \frac{1}{6}$
2: $3|x - 2| < \frac{1}{2}$
3: $|3x - 6| < \frac{1}{2}$
4: $|(3x + 1) - 7| < \frac{1}{2}$

We have shown that if x is within a distance of $\frac{1}{6}$ of 2, then $3x + 1$ is within a distance of $\frac{1}{2}$ of 7. Find a value for δ that will satisfy the statement

$$|x - 2| < \delta \Rightarrow |(3x + 1) - 7| < \frac{1}{4}$$

$\delta \leq \frac{1}{12}$. This upper limit on the values δ may assume was found by starting with the consequent, $|(3x + 1) - 7| < \frac{1}{4}$, and changing it until we had a statement similar to the antecedent, $|x - 2| < \delta$.

Exploration:

A: $|(3x + 1) - 7| < \frac{1}{4}$
B: $|3x - 6| < \frac{1}{4}$
C: $3|x - 2| < \frac{1}{4}$
D: $|x - 2| < \frac{1}{12}$

Therefore, if we let δ be any positive real number less than or equal to $\frac{1}{12}$, we can prove that

$$|x - 2| < \delta \Rightarrow |(3x + 1) - 7| < \frac{1}{4}$$

——

3 - 9 : What values of δ will satisfy the statement

$$|x - 2| < \delta \Rightarrow |(3x + 1) - 7| < 0.01?$$

——

$\delta \leq 0.0033$

Exploration:

A: $|(3x + 1) - 7| < 0.01$
B: $|3x - 6| < 0.01$
C: $3|x - 2| < 0.01$
D: $|x - 2| < 0.0033$

Notice that step C does not imply step D, since $0.0033 < 0.01/3$. However, D does imply C, and this is what is important in the proof that

$$|x - 2| < 0.0033 \Rightarrow |(3x + 1) - 7| < 0.01$$

Proof:

1: $|x - 2| < 0.0033$
2: $3|x - 2| < 0.01$
3: $|3x - 6| < 0.01$
4: $|(3x + 1) - 7| < 0.01$

So we see that we could have chosen any number less than $0.01/3$. $\delta = 0.0003$, $\delta = 0.0001$, or $\delta = 0.0009$ are some of the infinite number of values δ may assume. It is important to realize that in the exploration one is looking for a next step that will imply the step already written. There are usually an infinite number of possibilities for the next step, but fortunately one or two are more obvious.

If C is $3|x - 2| < 0.01$, then

D: $|x - 2| < 0.0001$

is acceptable; so is

D: $|x - 2| < 10^{-6}$

but the D statement that seems most natural is

D: $|x - 2| < 0.0033$

It is important that $D \Rightarrow C$ but not necessary that $C \Rightarrow D$.

---

3 - 10 : Prove that the function $\{(x, y)|y = 3x + 1, x \in \text{Re}\}$ is continuous at the point 3 in its domain. This is the first proof you have been asked to write, so take this frame very seriously. You should check the definition in frame 3-7 and write an exploration before attempting the proof. Please consider this frame a challenge rather than an impossible hurdle.

We must prove that
   for each positive real number ε
   there exists a positive real number δ
     such that
   for each x in the domain of $\{(x, 3x + 1)\}$
   $|x - 3| < \delta \Rightarrow |(3x + 1) - 10| < \varepsilon$

Exploration:

A: $|(3x + 1) - 10| < \varepsilon$

B: $|3x - 9| < \varepsilon$

C: $|x - 3| < \dfrac{\varepsilon}{3}$

This last statement is simply the antecedent

$$|x - 3| < \delta \quad \text{if } \delta = \frac{\varepsilon}{3}$$

Proof that $\{(x, y)|y = 3x + 1,\ x \in \text{Re}\}$ is continuous at the point 3 in its domain:

1: For any given ε, choose $\delta = \varepsilon/3$.

2: If $|x - 3| < \delta$, then

3: $|x - 3| < \dfrac{\varepsilon}{3}$

4: $|3x - 9| < \varepsilon$

5: $|(3x + 1) - 10| < \varepsilon$

Therefore,

6: $|x - 3| < \delta \Rightarrow |(3x + 1) - 10| < \varepsilon$

3-11 : Prove that $f = \{(x, y)|y = 3x + 1,\ x \in \text{Re}\}$ is continuous at 1.

We must prove that
  for each positive real number ε
  there exists a positive real number δ
    such that
  for each x in the domain of $\{(x, 3x + 1)\}$
  $|x - 1| < \delta \Rightarrow |(3x + 1) - 4| < \varepsilon$

Exploration:

A: $|(3x + 1) - 4| < \varepsilon$
B: $|3x - 3| < \varepsilon$

C: $|x - 1| < \dfrac{\varepsilon}{3}$

Proof:

1: For any given ε, choose $\delta = \varepsilon/3$.
2: If $|x - 1| < \delta$, then

3: $|x - 1| < \dfrac{\varepsilon}{3}$

4: $3|x - 1| < \varepsilon$
5: $|3x - 3| < \varepsilon$
6: $|(3x + 1) - 4| < \varepsilon$

Therefore,

7: $|x - 1| < \delta \Rightarrow |(3x + 1) - 4| < \varepsilon$

By Definition 3-1 this is a proof that this function is continuous at 1 in its domain.

—————

3-12: Prove that $f = \{(x, y)|y = x^2 - 3x - 4, x \in \text{Re}\}$ is continuous at 3. It is important to keep in mind that the exploration is not a proof but a search for a place to start a proof. If we have a step in the exploration

C: $|x| \, |x - 3| < \varepsilon$

then the next step can be any statement which might imply that $|x| \, |x - 3| < \varepsilon$. If we are restricting the values of x to a neighborhood of radius 1 about 3, $x \in N_1(3)$, then $2 < x < 4$ and $|x| < 4$. So we know that

D: $4|x - 3| < \varepsilon$

will imply C.   So will

D: $5|x - 3| < \varepsilon$

or

D: $100|x - 3| < \varepsilon$

─────

We must show that
   for each positive real number ε
   there exists a positive real number δ
     such that
   for each x in the domain of f
   $|x - 3| < \delta \Rightarrow |(x^2 - 3x - 4) - (-4)| < \varepsilon$

Exploration:

A: $|(x^2 - 3x - 4) - (-4)| < \varepsilon$
B: $|x^2 - 3x| < \varepsilon$
C: $|x|\,|x - 3| < \varepsilon$
D: $4|x - 3| < \varepsilon$ if $x \in N_1(3)$
E: $|x - 3| < \dfrac{\varepsilon}{4}$

    In step D we can substitute 4 for $|x|$ because if $x \in N_1(3)$, then $|x|$ is never greater than 4.   We must substitute the largest possible value for $|x|$ since we want D to imply C in the proof.

Proof:

1: For any given ε, choose δ to be the smaller of $\varepsilon/4$ and 1; i.e., choose $\delta = \min\{\varepsilon/4,\ 1\}$ (that is, $\delta = $ minimum of $\varepsilon/4$ and 1).
2: If $|x - 3| < \delta$, then
3: $|x - 3| < \dfrac{\varepsilon}{4}$ and $|x - 3| < 1$
4: $4|x - 3| < \varepsilon$ and $3 - 1 < x < 3 + 1$
5: $4|x - 3| < \varepsilon$ and $2 < x < 4$

6: $4|x - 3| < \varepsilon$ and $|x| < 4$

7: $|x| \, |x - 3| < \varepsilon$

Since 6 states that $|x| < 4$, then $4|x - 3| < \varepsilon$ implies that $|x| \, |x - 3| < \varepsilon$.

8: $|x^2 - 3x| < \varepsilon$

9: $|(x^2 - 3x - 4) - (-4)| < \varepsilon$

Therefore,

10: $|x - 3| < 8 \Rightarrow |(x^2 - 3x - 4) - (-4)| < \varepsilon$

Steps 1 to 10 show that

    for each positive real number ε

    there exists a positive real number $\delta = \min \{\varepsilon/4, \, 1\}$

        such that

    for each x in the domain of $\{(x, \, x^2 - 3x - 4)\}$

    $|x - 3| < \delta \Rightarrow |(x^2 - 3x - 4) - (-4) < \varepsilon$

which is the statement that $\{(x, \, x^2 - 3x - 4)\}$ is continuous at 3.

3-13 : Prove that $f = \{(x, \, y)|y = x^2 - 3x - 4, \, x \in \mathrm{Re}\}$ is continuous at 2.

We must show that

    for each positive real number ε

    there exists a positive real number δ

        such that

    for each x in the domain of f

    $|x - 2| < \delta \Rightarrow |(x^2 - 3x - 4) - (-6)| < \varepsilon$

Exploration:

A: $|(x^2 - 3x - 4) - (-6)| < \varepsilon$

B: $|x^2 - 3x + 2| < \varepsilon$

C: $|x - 1| \, |x - 2| < \varepsilon$

D: $2|x - 2| < \varepsilon$ if $\delta \leq 1$

E: $|x - 2| < \dfrac{\varepsilon}{2}$

In step D we substituted 2 for $|x - 1|$ because $|x - 1|$ is never larger than 2 if x is in a neighborhood of radius 1 about the point 2. In other words, we say that if $1 < x < 3$, then $0 < x - 1 < 2$.

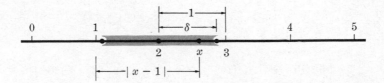

We do not insist that C imply D but that D imply C. If the "big" quantity $2|x - 2|$ is less than ε, then the "small" quantity $|x - 1|\,|x - 2|$ is less than ε.

Proof:

1: For a given ε, choose δ to be the smaller of ε/2 and 1; that is, $\delta = \min\{\varepsilon/2,\, 1\}$.

2: If $|x - 2| < \delta$, then

3: $|x - 2| < \dfrac{\varepsilon}{2}$ and $\quad |x - 2| < 1$

4: $2|x - 2| < \varepsilon$ and $\quad 2 - 1 < x < 2 + 1$

5: $2|x - 2| < \varepsilon$ and $\quad 0 < x - 1 < 2$

6: $2|x - 2| < \varepsilon$ and $\quad |x - 1| < 2$

Because 6 states that $|x - 1| < 2$, we may substitute $|x - 1|$ for 2 in $2|x - 2| < \varepsilon$, since the substitution will make the left-hand side of the inequality even smaller.

7: $|x - 1|\,|x - 2| < \varepsilon$

8: $|x^2 - 3x + 2| < \varepsilon$

9: $|(x^2 - 3x - 4) - (-6)| < \varepsilon$

Therefore,

10: $|x - 2| < \delta \Rightarrow |(x^2 - 3x - 4) - (-6)| < \varepsilon$

3-14 : If you were given an ε of 0.01, what value of δ could you choose to ensure that the conditions in 3-13 are satisfied?

δ ≤ 0.005, since 0.01/2 = 0.005. Notice that $|x - 2| < 0.005 \Rightarrow$ $|f(x) - f(2)| < 0.01$. *Check:* Let $x = 2.004$. Then $|2.004 - 2|$ < 0.005 and $|(2.004^2 - 3(2.004) - 4) - (-6)| = 0.004016 <$ 0.01.

3-15 : Prove that $\{(x, y)|y = x^2 - x - 12, x \in \text{Re}\}$ is continuous at 5.

We show that
    for each positive real number ε
    there exists a positive real number δ
        such that
    for each x in the domain of $\{(x, x^2 - x - 12)\}$
    $|x - 5| < δ \Rightarrow |(x^2 - x - 12) - 8| < ε$
To save time, we shall dispense with the exploration and give the proof directly. The student can discover our exploration by taking the steps of the proof in reverse order.

Proof:

  1: For each ε, choose $δ = \min\{ε/10, 1\}$, that is, the smaller of $ε/10$ and 1.

  2: If $|x - 5| < δ$, then

  3: $|x - 5| < \dfrac{ε}{10}$ and $|x - 5| < 1$

  4: $10|x - 5| < ε$ and $5 - 1 < x < 5 + 1$

  5: $10|x - 5| < ε$ and $8 < x + 4 < 10$

  6: $10|x - 5| < ε$ and $|x + 4| < 10$

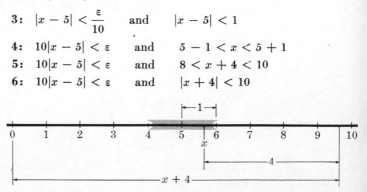

By substituting $|x + 4|$ for 10 in $10|x - 5| < \varepsilon$, we have

7: $|x + 4|\,|x - 5| < \varepsilon$

8: $|x^2 - x - 20| < \varepsilon$

9: $|(x^2 - x - 12) - 8| < \varepsilon$

Therefore,

10: $|x - 5| < \delta \Rightarrow |(x^2 - x - 12) - 8| < \varepsilon$

---

3 - 16 : Prove that $\{(x, y)|y = x^2 + 8x + 7, x \in \text{Re}\}$ is continuous at -7.

We must prove that

for each positive real number ε

there exists a positive real number δ

such that

for each x in the domain of $\{(x, x^2 + 8x + 7)\}$

$|x - (-7)| < \delta \Rightarrow |(x^2 + 8x + 7) - 0| < \varepsilon$

By an exploration which was similar to the following proof in reverse, we found that if we choose δ to be the smaller of $\varepsilon/7$ and 1, then the above statement is true.

Proof:

1: For each ε, choose $\delta = \min\{\varepsilon/7, 1\}$.

2: If $|x - (-7)| < \delta$, then

3: $|x - (-7)| < \dfrac{\varepsilon}{7}$ and $|x - (-7)| < 1$

4: $|x + 7| < \dfrac{\varepsilon}{7}$ and $-7 - 1 < x < -7 + 1$

5: $7|x + 7| < \varepsilon$ and $-7 < x + 1 < -5$

6: $7|x + 7| < \varepsilon$ and $|x + 1| < 7$

If we substitute $|x + 1|$ for 7 in $7|x + 7| < \varepsilon$, we have

7: $\quad |x + 1|\,|x + 7| < \varepsilon$

8: $\quad |(x^2 + 8x + 7) - 0| < \varepsilon$

9: $\quad$ Therefore, we have proved that for each ε, if we choose $\delta = \min\{\varepsilon/7, 1\}$, then $|x - (-7)| < \delta \Rightarrow |(x^2 + 8x + 7) - 0| < \varepsilon$. This is a proof that $\{(x, y)|y = x^2 + 8x + 7, x \in \text{Re}\}$ is continuous at -7.

3 - 17 : What value of δ could you choose to show that
$$|x - (-7)| < \delta \Rightarrow |(x^2 + 8x + 7) - 0| < 7\tfrac{7}{220}?$$

$\delta \leq \tfrac{1}{20}$, since $7\tfrac{7}{220}/7 = 1\tfrac{1}{220} = \tfrac{1}{20}$.

Some of the explorations may seem mystical or tricky to the reader who is discovering them for the first time. Keep in mind that the exploration starts with $|f(x) - f(c)| < \varepsilon$; by substituting any value or formula that will make the left side of the inequality larger than or equal to its value in the previous step, we end up with $|x - c| < \delta$. Remember: the steps of the exploration are the steps of the proof in reverse order.

The proof is always a conditional proof, which asserts that *if $|x - c| < \delta$, then $|f(x) - f(c)| < \varepsilon$.*

3 - 18 : Prove that $f = \{(x, y)|y = (x^2 + x - 6)/(x^2 - 4), x \in \text{Re}, x \neq 2, x \neq -2\}$ is continuous at 3.

We must show that
for each positive real number ε
there exists a positive real number δ
such that

for each x in the domain of f

$$|x - 3| < \delta \Longrightarrow \left| \frac{x^2 + x - 6}{x^2 - 4} - \frac{6}{5} \right| < \varepsilon$$

For a given ε, we can find a δ by the following exploration:

Exploration:

A: $\left| \dfrac{x^2 + x - 6}{x^2 - 4} - \dfrac{6}{5} \right| < \varepsilon$

B: $\left| \dfrac{(x + 3)(x - 2)}{(x + 2)(x - 2)} - \dfrac{6}{5} \right| < \varepsilon$

C: $\left| \dfrac{5x + 15 - 6x - 12}{5(x + 2)} \right| < \varepsilon$

D: $\dfrac{|3 - x|}{|x + 2|} < 5\varepsilon$

E: $\dfrac{|x - 3|}{4} < 5\varepsilon$ if $x \in N_1(3)$

F: $|x - 3| < 20\varepsilon$

In statement E, if we restrict δ to a maximum value of 1 [so that $x \in N_1(3)$], then $2 < x < 4$ and $4 < x + 2 < 6$, so that $|x + 2| > 4$. Therefore, statement E, $|x - 3|/4 < 5\varepsilon$, will imply statement D, $|x - 3|/|x + 2| < 5\varepsilon$, and the exploration in reverse order becomes a proof.

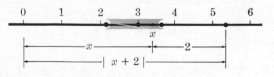

Proof:

1: For a given ε, choose $\delta = \min \{20\varepsilon, 1\}$.

2: If $|x - 3| < \delta$, then

3: $|x - 3| < 20\varepsilon$ and $|x - 3| < 1$

4: $\dfrac{|x - 3|}{20} < \varepsilon$ and $3 - 1 < x < 3 + 1$

5: $\dfrac{|x-3|}{(5)(4)} < \varepsilon$ and $4 < x + 2 < 6$

6: $\dfrac{|x-3|}{(5)(4)} < \varepsilon$ and $|x + 2| > 4$

Since $|x + 2| > 4$, we may substitute it for 4 in $|x - 3|/(5)(4) < \varepsilon$, as the substitution will simply make the left-hand side of the inequality smaller.

7: $\dfrac{|x-3|}{5|x+2|} < \varepsilon$

8: $\left| \dfrac{5x + 15 - 6x - 12}{5(x+2)} \right| < \varepsilon$

9: $\left| \dfrac{x+3}{x+2} - \dfrac{6}{5} \right| < \varepsilon$

10: $\left| \dfrac{(x+3)(x-2)}{(x+2)(x-2)} - \dfrac{6}{5} \right| < \varepsilon$

11: $\left| \dfrac{x^2 + x - 6}{x^2 - 4} - \dfrac{6}{5} \right| < \varepsilon$

Therefore, for every ε we have found a $\delta = \min\{20\varepsilon, 1\}$ such that

$$|x - 3| < \delta \Rightarrow \left| \dfrac{x^2 + x - 6}{x^2 - 4} - \dfrac{6}{5} \right| < \varepsilon$$

This is all that is required for the function to be continuous at the point 3.

———

3-19 : If we are given $\varepsilon = 0.001$, what value of δ will assure that if $x \in N_\delta(3)$, then $f(x) \in N_\varepsilon(\%)$, for the function of frame 3-18?

———

$\delta \leq 0.02$

———

3-20 : Graph $\{(x, y)|y = (x^2 + x - 6)/(x^2 - 4), x \neq 2, x \neq -2,$
$x \in \text{Re}\}$.

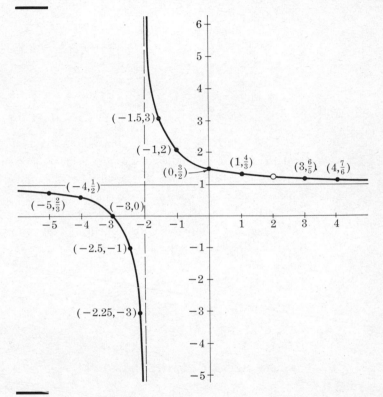

3-21 : Prove that $f = \{(x, y)|y = (x^2 + x - 6)/(x^2 - 4), x \in \text{Re},$
$x \neq 2, x \neq -2\}$ is continuous at -2.5 in its domain.

We must show that
   for each positive real number ε
   there exists a positive real number δ
      such that
   for each x in the domain of f
$$|x - (-2.5)| < \delta \Rightarrow \left| \frac{x^2 + x - 6}{x^2 - 4} - (-1) \right| < \varepsilon$$

Exploration:

A: $\left| \dfrac{x^2 + x - 6}{x^2 - 4} - (-1) \right| < \varepsilon$

B: $\left| \dfrac{(x + 3)(x - 2)}{(x + 2)(x - 2)} + 1 \right| < \varepsilon$

C: $\left| \dfrac{x + 3}{x + 2} + 1 \right| < \varepsilon$

D: $\dfrac{|2x + 5|}{|x + 2|} < \varepsilon$

If we look at the graph of the function (frame 3-20), we notice that the function is unbounded in any neighborhood of -2. It is necessary that -2 not be in any δ-neighborhood of -2.5 which we might choose to satisfy some ε-restriction. We must restrict the values of x to some neighborhood of -2.5 which does not include -2 and in which f is bounded. Any radius less than $\frac{1}{2}$ will do. Let us restrict $x \in N_{\frac{1}{4}}(-2.5)$ so that we shall know we are safe.

If $x \in N_{\frac{1}{4}}(-2.5)$, then

$-1\frac{1}{4} < x < -\frac{3}{4}$
$-\frac{3}{4} < x + 2 < -\frac{1}{4}$
$|x + 2| > \frac{1}{4}$

Therefore, one choice for E is

E: $\dfrac{2|x + 2.5|}{\frac{1}{4}}$

We could have made the restriction $x \in N_{0.1}(-2.5)$. Then

$-2.6 < x < -2.4$
$-0.6 < x + 2 < -0.4$
$|x + 2| > 0.4$

Then E would be

E: $\dfrac{2|x + 2.5|}{0.4} < \varepsilon$

F: $|x - (-2.5)| < 0.2\varepsilon$

G: Choose $\delta = \min \{0.2\varepsilon, 0.1\}$.

In other words, we can restrict x to be in any neighborhood of -2.5 whose radius is less than $\frac{1}{2}$. We shall continue the exploration and proof with the restriction that $x \in N_{1/4}(-2.5)$.

E: $\dfrac{2|x + 2.5|}{\frac{1}{4}} < \varepsilon$

F: $2|x - (-2.5)| < \dfrac{\varepsilon}{4}$

G: $|x - (-2.5)| < \dfrac{\varepsilon}{8}$

H: Choose $\delta = \min \{\varepsilon/8, \frac{1}{4}\}$.

Proof:

1: For any given ε, choose $\delta = \min \{\varepsilon/8, \frac{1}{4}\}$.

2: If $|x - (-2.5)| < \delta$, then

3: $|x + (2.5)| < \dfrac{\varepsilon}{8}$ and $|x + 2.5| < \frac{1}{4}$

4: $2|x + 2.5| < \dfrac{\varepsilon}{4}$ and $-1\frac{1}{4} < x < -\frac{3}{4}$

5: $\dfrac{|2x + 5|}{\frac{1}{4}} < \varepsilon$ and $-\frac{3}{4} < x + 2 < -\frac{1}{4}$

6: $\dfrac{|2x + 5|}{\frac{1}{4}} < \varepsilon$ and $|x + 2| > \frac{1}{4}$

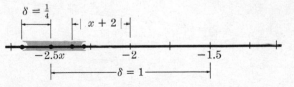

If we substitute $|x + 2|$ for $\frac{1}{4}$ in $|2x + 5|/\frac{1}{4} < \varepsilon$, we have

7: $\left|\dfrac{2x + 5}{x + 2}\right| < \varepsilon$

8: $\left|\dfrac{x + 3}{x + 2} + 1\right| < \varepsilon$

9: $\left| \dfrac{(x+3)(x-2)}{(x+2)(x-2)} - (-1) \right| < \varepsilon \qquad x - 2 \neq 0$

since $x \neq 2$

10: $\left| \dfrac{x^2 + x - 6}{x^2 - 4} - (-1) \right| < \varepsilon$

Therefore, f is continuous at -2.5.

3-22 : If we are given $\varepsilon = 0.001$ in 3-21, what value of δ will assure us that if $x \in N_\delta(-2.5)$, then $f(x) \in N_\varepsilon(-1)$?

$\delta \leq 0.000125$. Notice that at 3 in the domain δ may be twenty times as big as ε, but at -2.5 in the domain δ may be only one-eighth as large as ε.

Look at the graph of the function

$$f = \left\{ (x, y)\,\middle|\, y = \frac{x^2 + x - 6}{x^2 - 4}, \ x \in \mathrm{Re}, \ x \neq 2, -2 \right\}$$

near the point 3 (Fig. 3-6). Our exploration in 3-18 tells us that a $\delta = 20\varepsilon$ will ensure that $|f(x) - f(3)| < \varepsilon$. If $\varepsilon = \frac{1}{2}$, then δ can be 10. If $\varepsilon = \frac{1}{40}$, then $\delta \leq \frac{1}{2}$. In

Figure 3-6

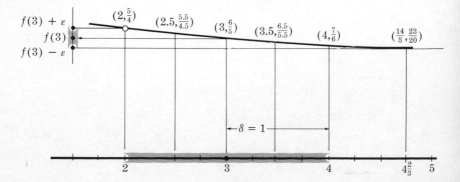

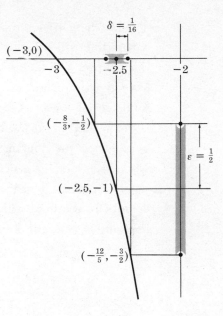

Figure 3-7

the graph of the function near -2.5 (Fig. 3-7), the restriction on δ for a given ε is much more stringent. Even with a large $\varepsilon = \frac{1}{2}$, the δ chosen is only $\frac{1}{16}$. However, if $|x - (-2.5)| < \varepsilon/8$, then $|f(x) - f(-2.5)| < \varepsilon$.

3-23: Is $f = \{(x, y)|y = (x^2 + x - 6)/(x^2 - 4),\ x \in \text{Re},\ x \neq 2,$
$x \neq -2\}$ continuous at 2?

No, since we have defined continuity only at points of the domain, and 2 is not in the domain of f.

3-24: Is $f = \{(x, y)|y = (x^2 + x - 6)/(x^2 - 4),\ x \in \text{Re},\ x \neq 2,$
$x \neq -2\}$ continuous at -2?

No. Again, -2 is not in the domain of f.

In Chap. 2 we discussed limits of a sequence and gave a definition which led to the challenger-defender game. In this chapter we have discussed continuity at a point and have given a definition which leads to the same game. It would seem, since the sequence is a function whose domain is the natural numbers, that if we generalize this definition by allowing the domain of the function to be all the real numbers, we might generate a definition of limit of a function at a point. This is almost true, and we shall develop a definition for a limit which will be very useful in discussing the points at which a function is not continuous.

Chapter Four: Limits

Throughout this study we have first discussed topics in an intuitive manner and then slowly progressed to the level of precision appropriate for clear communication. We have used many different approaches to limits and continuity, since this is the way the subject has developed historically.

In Fig. 4-1 we have graphed the function

$$\{(x, y)|y = 6x - x^2\}$$

and in order to study its behavior near the point (3, 9) we have pictured an enlargement of that portion of the curve which is framed between the lines $x = 2$, $x = 4$, $y = 10$, and $y = 8$.

To investigate the behavior of the function at points even closer to (3, 9), we have made an enlargement of the enlargement. Figure 4-1 also shows the second enlargement, which is framed by the lines $x = 2.5$, $x = 3.5$, $y = 8.25$, and $y = 9.75$. If we continue to make enlargements of the curve around the vertex of the parabola, we shall leave out many points of the function, but each frame will contain all points of the function defined on some neighborhood of 3. This is similar to saying that $6x - x^2$

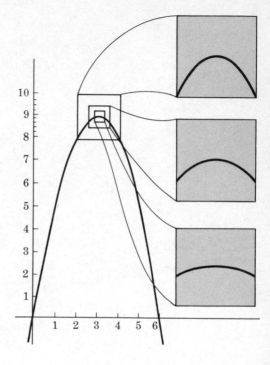

Figure 4-1

approaches 9 as x approaches 3, which we symbolize, $(6x - x^2) \rightarrow 9$ as $x \rightarrow 3$.

If we consider the height of a frame to be 2ε and the width of a frame to be 2δ, as shown in Fig. 4-2, then saying that every frame around the vertex of the parabola contains all points of the function in some neighborhood of 3 is equivalent to saying that the function is continuous at 3 in its domain. In fact some books define continuity at a point in just this manner.

A function f is continuous at a point b in its domain if and only if for every positive real number ε there

is a positive real number δ so that one can construct a frame of height 2ε and width 2δ centered on the point $(b, f(b))$ such that the graph of the function over the interval $(b - \delta;\ b + \delta)$ is a subset of the interior of the frame.

This definition simply insists that the curve enter the left vertical side of the frame and then pass out the right side of the frame without ever passing through the top or bottom of the frame.

This discussion about frames and limits might seem unnecessary, since we have already developed an ε,δ-definition for continuity which appears to be sufficient for describing the behavior of $6x - x^2$ in any frame. However, if we

Figure 4-2

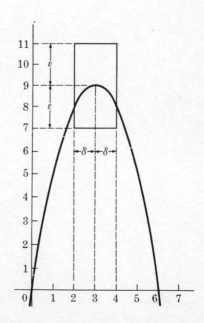

consider the limit of the function

$$f = \left\{ (x,\, y) \middle| y = \frac{x^2 - 9}{x - 3},\; x \neq 3 \right\}$$

as x approaches 3, we notice that it does not make sense to discuss $f(3)$ since the function is not defined at 3. Our definitions of continuity are applied only to points in the domain of the function, so they are not a proper vehicle for discussing the behavior of f about the point $(3, 6)$.

Figure 4-3 shows the graph of f along with enlargements of the points of the function about the point $(3, 6)$. The first enlargement is framed by the lines $x = 2$, $x = 4$, $y = 5$, and $y = 7$. Each of the enlargements looks the same as

Figure 4-3

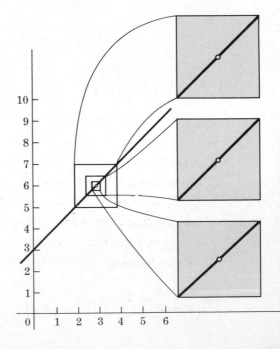

the previous enlargement. This sameness is intentional, to show that the point which is deleted does not have width. In other words no matter how many enlargements we make of this particular function, the resulting picture will look the same, since lines do not have width and points do not have dimension.

Consider the height of the side of a frame to be 2ε and the bottom of a frame to be 2δ in width. It is apparent that for any given ε-closeness to 6 in the range, we can choose $\delta = \varepsilon$ as a δ-closeness to 3 in the domain; and if x is within a δ-neighborhood of 3 but not equal to 3, then $f(x)$ is within an ε-neighborhood of 6. This would be the definition of "f is continuous at the point 3" if 3 were in the domain of f.

By adding the point $(3, 6)$ to f we create a new function $g = \{(x, y)|y = x + 3\}$ which is continuous at 3 in its domain. Our new function g was motivated by the fact that

$$\frac{x^2 - 9}{x - 3} = \frac{(x - 3)(x + 3)}{x - 3}$$

and if x is not 3, we can divide both the numerator and denominator by $x - 3$ to obtain the fact that the fraction is equal to $x + 3$ at all points on the real line except 3. It is not necessary that $(3, 6)$ be in the function f for f to have a limit at 3, but it is essential that the new function g, which does have the point $(3, 6)$, be continuous at 3. In other words if our function f can be made into a continuous function g by simply adding the point $(3, 6)$ we say that

$$\lim_{x \to 3} \frac{x^2 - 9}{x - 3} = 6$$

We can state this as a definition of a limit.

The real number L is the limit of $f(x)$ as x approaches b if and only if there exists a function g equal to f at all points in the domain of f except b, the point (b, L) is in g, and g is continuous at b.

Consider the function $h = \{(x, y)|y = 6x - x^2$ when $x < 3$, $y = 6x - x^2 + 1$ when $x > 3$, $x \neq 3\}$, which is graphed in Fig. 4-4 along with several enlargements about the point $(3, 9)$. Notice that some points of h to the left of $(3, 9)$ seem to be in every frame, but the points of h to the right of $(3, 9)$ are not in any of the smaller frames. It is *not* true that by adding the point $(3, 9)$ to h we shall obtain a continuous function at 3. Therefore, we cannot say that

Figure 4-4

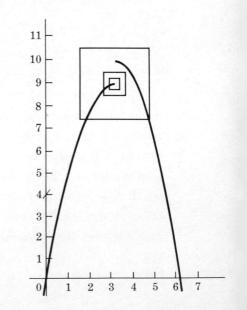

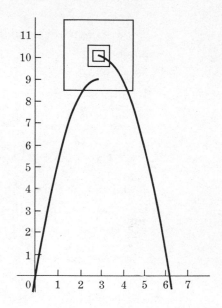

Figure 4-5

9 is the limit of $h(x)$ as x approaches 3.   We shall show later that we can say that the limit of $h(x)$ as x approaches 3 from the *left* is 9.

If we construct a set of frames about the point (3, 10) (Fig. 4-5), every frame contains points of h to the right of (3, 10), but the smaller frames do not contain any points of h to the left of (3, 10).   Again we cannot make h continuous at 3 by adding (3, 10), so we cannot say that 10 is the limit of $h(x)$ as x approaches 3, but we can say that 10 is the limit of $h(x)$ as x approaches 3 from the *right*.

If L is the limit of $f(x)$ as x approaches b from the left and L is also the limit of $f(x)$ as x approaches b from the right, then we can define a new function g which is the same as f at all points except at b and $g(b) = L$.   Since this new function g is continuous at b, we say that $\lim_{x \to b} f(x) = L$.

It is apparent that the limit of a function may exist at points that are not in the domain of the function. However, these points must be so close to the domain that any neighborhood of such a point will contain an infinite number of points of the domain of the function.

DEFINITION 4-1:

A point b will be called a *limit point* of a subset S of the real numbers if and only if every neighborhood of b contains a point of S other than b.

At first one might think that this definition does not require that every neighborhood of b contain an infinite number of points of S. If some neighborhood of b contains a *finite* number of points of S, then the closest of these points is a distance δ from b. So $N_\delta(b)$ contains no points of S. But this contradicts the assertion that b is a limit point of S, so there are an *infinite* number.

In Fig. 4-6 we have illustrated a function which is

Figure 4-6

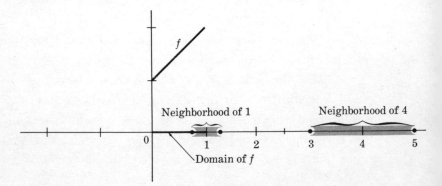

defined on the interval from 0 to 1. Let

$$f = \{(x, y)|y = x + 1, x \in (0; 1)\}$$

The limit points of the domain of the function are the points
0, 1, and all the points between 0 and 1. The point 4 is not
a limit point of the domain of f because the neighborhood
of radius 1 about 4 does not contain any points of the
domain of f.

DEFINITION 4-2:

**The real number L is the limit of $f(x)$ as x approaches
a limit point b of the domain of f if and only if**
    for each positive real number ε
    there exists a positive real number δ
        such that
    for each x in the domain of f
    if $0 < |x - b| < \delta$, then $|f(x) - L| < \varepsilon$.

    This definition of a limit looks very much like the defi-
nition of continuity at a point b, but it differs in three places.

1:   Whereas continuity is defined on the domain of the
    function, the limit is defined at limit points of the
    domain of the function.
2:   In the definition of continuity $|x - b| < \delta$ will allow x
    to be b, but in the definition of the limit $0 < |x - b| < \delta$
    will not allow x ever to become b.
3:   In the definition of continuity we have $|f(x) - f(b)| < \varepsilon$,
    but since the limit is also defined at points that are not
    in the domain of the function, we must substitute L for
    $f(b)$ in $|f(x) - f(b)| < \varepsilon$.

DEFINITION 3-1 (repeated):

A function f is continuous at a point b in the domain
of f if and only if
   for each positive real number ε
   there exists a positive real number δ
      such that
   for each x in the domain of f

$$|x - b| < \delta \Rightarrow |f(x) - f(b)| < \varepsilon$$

When discussing limits it will be necessary for us to
talk about deleted neighborhoods. The deleted neighbor-
hood $N_\delta^d(2)$ is the same as $N_\delta(2)$ except the point 2 has been
removed, as shown in Fig. 4-7.

We may not say that the function

$$f = \left\{ (x, y) \middle| y = \frac{x^2 - 4}{x - 2}, \; x \neq 2 \right\}$$

is continuous at the point 2, since the function f is not even
defined at 2. However, in every *deleted* neighborhood of 2
the fraction $(x^2 - 4)/(x - 2)$ is equal to $x + 2$. Thus we
can say that

$$\lim_{x \to 2} \frac{x^2 - 4}{x - 2} = \lim_{x \to 2} \frac{(x + 2)(x - 2)}{(x - 2)} = \lim_{x \to 2} (x + 2) = 4$$

since in the definition of the limit we do not allow x to be 2.

Figure 4-7

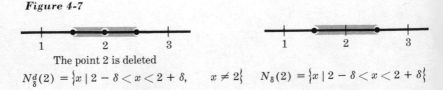

The point 2 is deleted

$$N_\delta^d(2) = \left\{ x \mid 2 - \delta < x < 2 + \delta, \quad x \neq 2 \right\} \qquad N_\delta(2) = \left\{ x \mid 2 - \delta < x < 2 + \delta \right\}$$

When we say that $\lim\limits_{x \to 2} (x + 2) = 4$, we are using the idea that $x + 2$ represents a function which is continuous at 2, so $\lim\limits_{x \to 2} (x + 2) = (2) + 2$; i.e., we can find the limit as x approaches 2 by substituting 2 for x in $x + 2$. This is often stated as a formal definition.

A function f is continuous at a point b in its domain if and only if $\lim\limits_{x \to b} f(x) = f(b)$.

If we had adopted this definition as our main definition of continuity in place of our ε, δ-definition, we should have defined the limit before we defined continuity. As the concept of limit is more difficult to understand, we chose to define continuity first. One often sees the above definition stated in the following form:

A function f is continuous at a point b if and only if
1: b is in the domain of f
2: $\lim\limits_{x \to b} f(x)$ exists
3: $\lim\limits_{x \to b} f(x) = f(b)$

If we wish to know the limit of $x + 3$ as x approaches 4 in the domain of the function $\{(x, y) | y = x + 3, x \in \text{Re}\}$, we ask, "What is the limit of $x + 3$ as x approaches 4?" In so doing we are assuming the reader will take for granted that the domain of the function is the real line. If the domain of the function f is not stated, it is understood to consist of the set of real numbers x for which $f(x)$ is defined.

4 - 1 : If a function f is continuous at c, then $\lim\limits_{x \to c} f(x) = f(c)$. To find the limit of $x + 3$ as $x \to 0$ we simply substitute 0 for x

in $x + 3$. $\lim\limits_{x \to 0} (x + 3) = 0 + 3$. What is $\lim\limits_{x \to 0} (2x + 3)$?

——

3, since $2(0) + 3 = 3$.

——

4-2: What is $\lim\limits_{x \to 4} \dfrac{x^2 - 16}{x - 4}$? This fraction is not defined at 4; however, the continuous function represented by $x + 4$ is equal to $(x^2 - 16)/(x - 4)$ at all points in any deleted neighborhood of 4.

——

8, since

$$\lim_{x \to 4} \frac{x^2 - 16}{x - 4} = \lim_{x \to 4} \frac{(x - 4)(x + 4)}{(x - 4)} = \lim_{x \to 4} (x + 4) = 8$$

——

4-3: What is $\lim\limits_{x \to 2} \dfrac{9x^2 - 36}{x - 2}$?

——

36, since

$$\lim_{x \to 2} \frac{9x^2 - 36}{x - 2} = \lim_{x \to 2} \frac{9(x - 2)(x + 2)}{x - 2} = \lim_{x \to 2} 9(x + 2) = 36$$

——

4-4: What is $\lim\limits_{x \to 2} \dfrac{x^2 - 4}{2x - 4}$?

——

2

——

4-5: What is $\lim\limits_{x \to 2} \dfrac{x^2 - 4}{2x - 2}$?

——

0. The function is continuous at 2, and $f(2) = 0$.

——

4 - 6 : What is $\lim\limits_{x \to 2} \dfrac{(2x)^2 - 4}{2x - 2}$?

_____

6. This function is continuous at 2, so the limit as x approaches 2 is $f(2)$.

4 - 7 : What is $\lim\limits_{x \to 1} \dfrac{(2x)^2 - 4}{2x - 2}$?

_____

4. The function is not continuous at 1, but

$$\lim_{x \to 1} \frac{(2x)^2 - 4}{2x - 2} = \lim_{x \to 1} \frac{4(x^2 - 1)}{2(x - 1)} = \lim_{x \to 1} 2(x + 1)$$

and $2(x + 1)$ is continuous at 1.

_____

4 - 8 : What is the limit of $(x^2 + x - 6)/(x^2 - 4)$ as x approaches 3? See frames 3-16 to 3-24.

_____

$\frac{6}{5}$

$$f(3) = \frac{(3)^2 + (3) - 6}{(3)^2 - 4} = \frac{6}{5}$$

_____

4 - 9 : What is $\lim\limits_{x \to -2.5} \dfrac{x^2 + x - 6}{x^2 - 4}$?

_____

−1. Again because the function is continuous at −2.5, the question is quite simple since $f(-2.5)$ is −1.

_____

4 - 10 : What is $\lim\limits_{x \to 2} \dfrac{x^2 + x - 6}{x^2 - 4}$?

_____

$\frac{5}{4}$. This seems reasonable since

$$\lim_{x \to 2} \frac{x^2 + x - 6}{x^2 - 4} = \lim_{x \to 2} \frac{(x - 2)(x + 3)}{(x - 2)(x + 2)} = \lim_{x \to 2} \frac{x + 3}{x + 2}$$

and $(x + 3/x + 2)$ is continuous at 2.

_____

4 - 1 1 : Prove that $\lim\limits_{x \to 2} \dfrac{x^2 + x - 6}{x^2 - 4} = \dfrac{5}{4}$.

We must prove that

    for each positive real number ε

    there exists a positive real number δ

        such that

    for each x in the domain of $\left\{ \left(x, \dfrac{x^2 + x - 6}{x^2 - 4} \right) \right\}$

    if $0 < |x - 2| < \delta$, then $\left| \dfrac{x^2 + x - 6}{x^2 - 4} - \dfrac{5}{4} \right| < \varepsilon$.

The following exploration is a search for such a δ in terms of the given ε.

Exploration:

We start with

A: $\quad \left| \dfrac{x^2 + x - \text{·}6}{x^2 - 4} - \dfrac{5}{4} \right| < \varepsilon$

and attempt to reduce the left side until it is similar to the antecedent, $0 < |x - 2| < \delta$. First we shall use the fact that $x \neq 2$ in dividing $x - 2$ out of both the numerator and denominator of $(x^2 + x - 6)/(x^2 - 4)$ to obtain

B: $\quad \left| \dfrac{x + 3}{x + 2} - \dfrac{5}{4} \right| < \varepsilon$

C: $\quad \left| \dfrac{4x + 12 - 5x - 10}{4(x + 2)} \right| < \varepsilon$

D: $\quad \dfrac{|-x + 2|}{4|x + 2|} < \varepsilon$

We are taking the limit as $x \to 2$, so if x is within a deleted neighborhood of radius 1 about 2, we know that $1 < x < 3$ and $3 < x + 2 < 5$. Since $x + 2$ is always greater than 3 in this neighborhood, we can substitute 3 for $x + 2$ in statement D.

E: $\dfrac{|x - 2|}{(4)(3)} < \varepsilon$

F: $|x - 2| < 12\varepsilon$

Proof:

1: For any given ε, choose δ to be the smaller of 1 and 12ε; that is, $\delta = \min\{12\varepsilon, 1\}$.

2: If $0 < |x - 2| < \delta$, then

3: $0 < |x - 2| < 12\varepsilon$ and $0 < |x - 2| < 1$

4: $\dfrac{|x - 2|}{(4)(3)} < \varepsilon$ and $1 < x < 3, \; x \neq 2$

5: $\dfrac{|x - 2|}{(4)(3)} < \varepsilon$ and $3 < x + 2 < 5$

6: $\dfrac{|x - 2|}{(4)(3)} < \varepsilon$ and $|x + 2| > 3$

If we substitute $|x + 2|$ for 3 in $|x - 2|/(4)(3) < \varepsilon$, we have

7: $\dfrac{|-x + 2|}{4|x + 2|} < \varepsilon$

8: $\left| \dfrac{4x + 12 - 5x - 10}{4(x + 2)} \right| < \varepsilon$

9: $\left| \dfrac{x + 3}{x + 2} - \dfrac{5}{4} \right| < \varepsilon$

10: $\left| \dfrac{x^2 + x - 6}{x^2 - 4} - \dfrac{5}{4} \right| < \varepsilon$ since $x - 2 \neq 0$

Therefore, we have proved that

for each ε

there is a $\delta = \min\{12\varepsilon, 1\}$

such that

for each x in the domain of $\left\{ x, \dfrac{x^2 + x - 6}{x^2 - 4} \right\}$

if $0 < |x - 2| < \delta$, then $\left| \dfrac{x^2 + x - 6}{x^2 - 4} - \dfrac{5}{4} \right| < \varepsilon.$

This is the exact definition of

$$\lim_{x \to 2} \frac{x^2 + x - 6}{x^2 - 4} = \frac{5}{4}$$

4-12 : In this frame we shall discuss the function which has the value −1 when $x < 0$, the value 0 when $x = 0$, and the value 1 when $x > 0$.

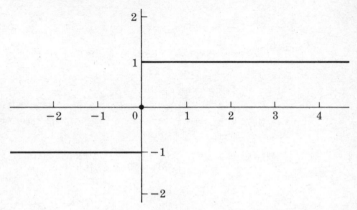

The limit as $x \to 0$ does not exist, since the points to the right of 0 map onto 1, whereas points to the left of 0 map onto −1. When this happens, we say that the limit as x approaches 0 from the right is 1, but the limit as x approaches 0 from the left is −1. If the limit as x approaches 0 from the right does not equal the limit as x approaches 0 from the left, we say that the limit does not exist. Does the limit as x approaches 0 from the right equal the limit as x approaches 0 from the left in the following function? The value of the function is 0 when $x \leq 0$ and is 1 when $x > 0$.

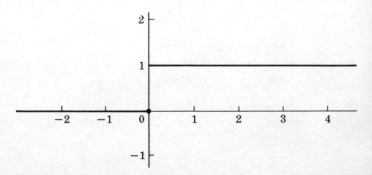

No. The limit as x approaches 0 from the left is 0, whereas the limit as x approaches 0 from the right is 1.

We shall symbolize "the limit of $f(x)$ as x approaches b from the right is L" as $\lim\limits_{x \to b+} f(x) = L$. Also $\lim\limits_{x \to b-} f(x) = L$ will be read "the limit of $f(x)$ as x approaches b from the left is L."

Figure 4-8 is a graph of the function represented by $(x^2 + x - 6)/(x^2 - 4)$. Notice that as $x \to -2$ from the right, the values of the function seem to increase without bound. On the other hand, as x approaches -2 from the left, the values of the function seem to decrease without bound. So the function is not only discontinuous at the point, but the limit as x approaches -2 does not exist.

We can define a limit as x approaches -2 from the right. $\lim\limits_{x \to -2+} \dfrac{x^2 + x - 6}{x^2 - 4} = +\infty$ if and only if

Figure 4-8

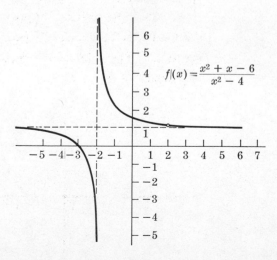

$$f(x) = \frac{x^2 + x - 6}{x^2 - 4}$$

for each positive real number M

there exists a positive real number δ

  such that

for each x in the domain of $\left\{\left(x, \dfrac{x^2 + x - 6}{x^2 - 4}\right)\right\}$

if $0 < (x - (-2)) < \delta$, then $f(x) > M$.

The new idea introduced here is that the fraction $(x^2 + x - 6)/(x^2 - 4)$ is very large at points near -2 on the right. The symbolism $\lim\limits_{x \to b} f(x) = +\infty$ means that $f(x)$ is increasing without bound as $x \to b$. Similarly, the symbolism $\lim\limits_{x \to b} f(x) = -\infty$ means that $f(x)$ is decreasing without bound as $x \to b$.

Figure 4-9

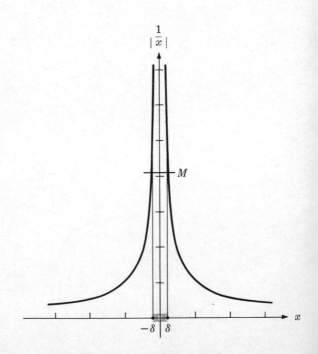

This is an easily minunderstood concept, so we shall use a simpler example to explore it a little further. Consider the fraction $1/|x|$, graphed in Fig. 4-9. The fraction is undefined when x is 0, but as x approaches 0 from either side, the fraction increases without bound.

Suppose we are required to make $1/|x|$ greater than 17. If we substitute $\frac{1}{18}$ for x in $1/|x|$, then it is equal to 18, which is larger than 17. Of course, if we substitute $-\frac{1}{18}$ in $1/|x|$, it will also be greater than 17. If we are asked to make $1/|x|$ greater than 1,000,000, then any substitution of an x value closer to 0 than 1/1,000,000 will make $1/|x|$ greater than 1,000,000.

4-13 : We can define the limit of $1/|x|$ as x approaches 0.
$\lim\limits_{x \to 0} 1/|x| = +\infty$ if and only if
> for each positive real number M
> there exists a positive real number δ
>> such that
> for each x in the domain of $\{(x,\ 1/|x|)\}$
> if $0 < |x - 0| < \delta$, then $1/|x| > M$.

Define the limit of $(x^2 + x - 6)/(x^2 - 4)$ as x approaches -2 from the left.

$\lim\limits_{x \to -2-} \dfrac{x^2 + x - 6}{x^2 - 4} = -\infty$ if and only if
> for each positive real number M
> there exists a positive real number δ
>> such that
> for each x in the domain of $\left\{\left(x, \dfrac{x^2 + x - 6}{x^2 - 4}\right)\right\}$
> if $0 < (-2 - x) < \delta$, then $f(x) < -M$.

The symbolism $0 < |x - b| < \delta$ will allow x to approach b from either side. In this definition we used $0 < (-2 - x) < \delta$ instead of $0 < |-2 - x| < \delta$ because we wanted to discuss the behavior of the fraction as x approached -2 only from the left.

4 - 14 : $\lim\limits_{x \to b-} f(x) = +\infty$ if and only if

for each positive real number M

there exists a positive real number δ

such that

for each x in the domain of f

if _____, then _____.

If $0 < (b - x) < \delta$, then $f(x) > M$. If x approaches b from the right, then the antecedent is $0 < (x - b) < \delta$. If x approaches b from the left, then the antecedent is $0 < (b - x) < \delta$. If x approaches b, then the antecedent is $0 < |x - b| < \delta$.

4 - 15 : $\lim\limits_{x \to b+} f(x) = -\infty$ if and only if

for each positive real number M

there exists a positive real number δ

such that

for each x in the domain of f

if _____, then _____.

If $0 < (x - b) < \delta$, then $f(x) < -M$. When we wish to say that a function becomes large without bound, we say that the limit is equal to $+\infty$. If the function is decreasing without bound, we say that the limit is equal to $-\infty$.

4 - 16 : $\lim\limits_{x \to b-} f(x) = +\infty$ if and only if

for each positive real number M

there exists a positive real number δ

such that

for each x in the domain of f

if _____, then _____.

If $0 < (b - x) < \delta$, then $f(x) > M$. This is how we state that the function increases without bound as x approaches b from the left. When x approaches b from the left, we subtract x from b, and when x approaches b from the right, we subtract b from x. We are no longer taking the absolute value of $x - b$ since that would insist that x be close to b on both sides. It is important that $x - b$ and $b - x$ be positive, so we must use $x - b$ when x is approaching b from the right and $b - x$ when x is approaching b from the left.

4-17 : $\displaystyle\lim_{x \to b-} f(x) = -\infty$ if and only if

for each positive real number M

there exists a positive real number δ

such that

for each x in the domain of f

if _____, then _____.

If $0 < b - x < \delta$, then $f(x) < -M$.

4-18 : $\displaystyle\lim_{x \to b} f(x) = +\infty$ if and only if

for each positive real number M

there exists a positive real number δ

such that

for each x in the domain of f

if _____, then _____.

If $0 < |x - b| < \delta$, then $f(x) > M$.

4-19 : $\lim\limits_{x \to b} f(x) = -\infty$ if and only if

for each positive real number M

there exists a positive real number δ

such that

for each x in the domain of f

if _____, then _____.

If $0 < |x - b| < \delta$, then $f(x) < -M$.

4-20 : What is the limit of $1/x$ as x approaches 0?

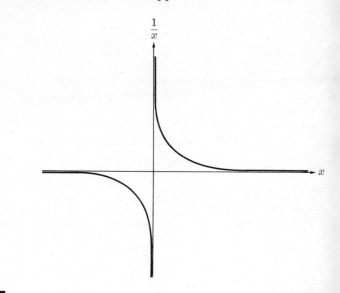

Undefined. The limit is not defined by our definition, since the limit from the left does not equal the limit from the right.

4-21 : What is the limit of $1/x$ as x approaches zero from the right?

$\lim\limits_{x \to 0+} 1/x = +\infty$. We can view this as a contest between M

and $f(x)$ to see which can become the larger. For any large number M one can find a small number δ such that if x is δ-close to zero on the right, then $1/x$ is larger than M. When we assert that the function increases without bound, we are asserting that it becomes bigger than any positive number we wish to name. When we assert that a function f is decreasing without bound, we mean that $f(x)$ is less than the negative of any large positive number we might name.

———

4 - 2 2 : What is the limit of $1/x$ as x approaches 0 from the left?

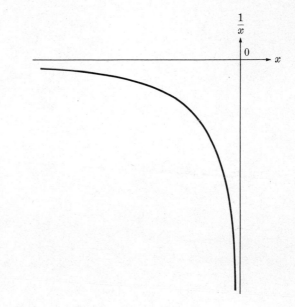

———

$$\lim_{x \to 0-} 1/x = -\infty$$

———

4 - 2 3 : What is the limit of $1/x$ as x approaches 3?

———

⅓

———

4 - 2 4 : What is the limit of $1/x$ as x increases without bound?

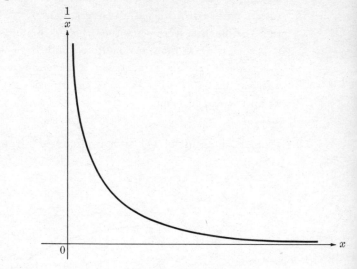

lim $1/x = 0$, since for every $\varepsilon > 0$ there exists an $N > 0$ such
$x \to +\infty$
that if $x > N$, then $|1/x - 0| < \varepsilon$.

4 - 2 5 : What is the limit of $1/x$ as x decreases without bound?

lim $1/x = 0$, since for each $\varepsilon > 0$ there exists an $N > 0$ such
$x \to -\infty$
that if $x < -N$, then $|1/x - 0| < \varepsilon$.

It is important that the symbols $+\infty$ and $-\infty$ *not* be considered as real numbers.

4 - 2 6 : What is the limit of $(x + 4)/(x - 5)$ as x approaches 5?

Undefined

4-27 : What is the limit of $(x + 4)/(x - 5)$ as x approaches 5 from the right?

$\lim\limits_{x \to 5+} \dfrac{x + 4}{x - 5} = +\infty$. The numerator is close to 9, and the denominator close to 0 as x takes on values near 5 on the right. The fraction increases without bound as x takes on values close to 5 on its right.

4-28 : What is the limit of $(x + 4)/(x - 5)$ as x approaches 5 from the left?

$\lim\limits_{x \to 5-} \dfrac{x + 4}{x - 5} = -\infty$. The fraction is negative for values of x between -4 and 5 and decreases without bound for values approaching 5 from the left.

4-29 : What is the limit of $(x - 3)/(x + 2)$ as $x \to -2+$, $x \to -2-$, $x \to -2$?

$-\infty$, $+\infty$, undefined

The numerator of this fraction approaches -5 while the denominator is approaching 0. The fraction is decreasing without bound as x approaches -2 from the left, is increasing without bound as x approaches -2 from the right, and has no limit as x approaches -2 from both sides.

4-30 : Discuss the behavior of $(x^2 + 3)/(x^2 - x)$ as x approaches 1.

The numerator approaches 4 as x approaches 1, and as x approaches 1 from the right, the denominator is positive and approaches 0.

$\lim\limits_{x \to 1+} \dfrac{x^2 + 3}{x^2 - x} = +\infty$

As x approaches 1 from the left, the denominator is negative.

$$\lim_{x \to 1-} \frac{x^2 + 3}{x^2 - x} = -\infty$$

The limit of $(x^2 + 3)/(x^2 - x)$ as x approaches 1 is not defined.

4-31 : What is the limit of $(x^2 + x - 2)/(x + 2)$ as x approaches -2.

$$\lim_{x \to -2} \frac{x^2 + x - 2}{x + 2} = -3.$$ Both the numerator and denominator approach 0 as $x \to -2$. If we look at the continuous function represented by $x - 1$ which is equal to $[(x + 2)(x - 1)]/(x + 2)$ except when x is -2, we see that the limit is -3. Keep in mind that we are dealing with deleted neighborhoods of -2 in the domain of the function the fraction represents.

4-32 : What is the limit of $[(c + h)^3 - c^3]/h$ as h approaches 0? *Hint:*

$$\lim_{h \to 0} \frac{(c + h)^3 - c^3}{h} = \lim_{h \to 0} \frac{(c^3 + 3c^2h + 3ch^2 + h^3) - c^3}{h} =$$

$$\lim_{h \to 0} 3c^2 + 3ch + h^2$$

$$\lim_{h \to 0} \frac{(c + h)^3 - c^3}{h} = 3c^2.$$ The expression $3c^2 + 3ch + h^2$ represents a continuous function, and the limit as $h \to 0$ of a function which is continuous at 0 is $f(0)$. In this case $f(0)$ is

$$3c^2 + 3c(0) + 0^2 = 3c^2$$

4-33 : What is the limit of $[(c + h)^2 - c^2]/h$ as h approaches 0? Proceed as in frame 4-32.

$$\lim_{h \to 0} \frac{(c + h)^2 - c^2}{h} = \lim_{h \to 0} \frac{(c^2 + 2ch + h^2) - c^2}{h} = \lim_{h \to 0} 2c + h = 2c$$

---

4 - 3 4 : What is the limit as x approaches $+\infty$ in $6/(x - 3)$?

0. If we test values like 1, 10, 100, 1,000, 10,000, . . . , then the fraction becomes $6/-2$, $6/7$, $6/97$, $6/997$, $6/9,997$, $6/99,997$, ... It is apparent that this fraction comes very close to 0 as x increases without bound. To prove that $\lim\limits_{x \to +\infty} \dfrac{6}{x - 3} = 0$, we must show that

for each positive real number ε

there exists a positive real number N

such that

for each x in the domain of $\left\{\left(x, \dfrac{6}{x - 3}\right)\right\}$

$$x > N \Rightarrow \left| \frac{6}{x - 3} - 0 \right| < \varepsilon$$

This may be done by choosing $N = (6 + 3\varepsilon)/\varepsilon$.

4 - 3 5 : What is the limit as x approaches $-\infty$ in $6/(x - 3)$?

0. If we test the negatives of the same values of x as above, we have $6/-4$, $6/-13$, $6/-103$, $6/-1,003$, $6/-10,003$, . . . , and we are apparently approaching 0. To prove that $\lim\limits_{x \to -\infty} \dfrac{6}{x - 3} = 0$, we must show that

for each positive real number ε

there exists a positive real number N

such that

for each x in the domain of $\left\{\left(x, \dfrac{6}{x - 3}\right)\right\}$

$$x < -N \Rightarrow \left| \frac{6}{x - 3} - 0 \right| < \varepsilon$$

The choice $N = (6 - 3\varepsilon)/\varepsilon$ meets this requirement.

4-36 : What is $\lim\limits_{x \to -\infty} \dfrac{-4}{x^2 + 3}$?

0

4-37 : What is $\lim\limits_{x \to +\infty} \dfrac{4x^2 - 3x + 2}{3x^2 - 6x + 1}$?

$\frac{4}{3}$. Here both the numerator and denominator approach $+\infty$ as x approaches $+\infty$. If we divide both the numerator and denominator by x^2, we have the fraction $(4 - 3/x + 2/x^2)/(3 - 6/x + 1/x^2)$. As x increases without bound, this fraction becomes $\frac{4}{3}$.

4-38 : What is $\lim\limits_{x \to -\infty} \dfrac{4x^2 - 3x + 2}{3x^2 - 6x + 1}$?

$\frac{4}{3}$. If one divides both the numerator and denominator by x^2, as above, and then takes the limit, it will be $\frac{4}{3}$. It is permissible to divide by x^2 as long as x is not 0, and if x is decreasing without bound, it is not 0.

4-39 : What is $\lim\limits_{x \to +\infty} \dfrac{5x^2 - 3x}{2x^3 + 2x}$?

---

0. If one divides both numerator and denominator by x^3, one has $(5/x - 3/x^2)/(2 + 2/x^2)$, which approaches 0 when x increases without bound.

4-40 : What is $\lim\limits_{x \to +\infty} \dfrac{x^2 - 3}{3 - x^2}$?

-1

4-41 : What is $\lim\limits_{x \to -\infty} \dfrac{x^6 - 3x^5 - 4x^4 - 2x^3 - x - 1}{3x^6 + 4x^5 - 3x^4 - 2x^3 - 2x - 9}$?

——

$\frac{1}{3}$. If one divides by x^6 in both numerator and denominator, it is only the coefficients of the highest-powered terms that affect the limit.

——

4-42 : What is $\lim\limits_{x \to +\infty} \dfrac{ax^n + bx^{n-1} + \cdots + h}{cx^m + dx^{m-1} + \cdots + p}$ if $n = m$?

——

a/c

——

4-43 : The algebraic identity $a^2 - b^2 = (a - b)(a + b)$ can be used to find the limit of some fractions with radical signs. If we are asked to find $\lim\limits_{h \to 0} \dfrac{\sqrt{4 + h} - \sqrt{4}}{h}$, we can use the above identity by letting $a = \sqrt{4 + h}$ and $b = \sqrt{4}$; then

$$\frac{\sqrt{4 + h} - \sqrt{4}}{h} \cdot \frac{\sqrt{4 + h} + \sqrt{4}}{\sqrt{4 + h} + \sqrt{4}} = \frac{(4 + h) - 4}{h(\sqrt{4 + h} + \sqrt{4})}$$

$$= \frac{h}{h(\sqrt{4 + h} + \sqrt{4})} = \frac{1}{\sqrt{4 + h} + \sqrt{4}}$$

This is an equivalent fraction, and

$$\lim\limits_{h \to 0} \frac{1}{\sqrt{4 + h} + \sqrt{4}} = \frac{1}{4}$$

What is $\lim\limits_{h \to 0} \dfrac{\sqrt{9 + h} - \sqrt{9}}{h}$? Let $a = \sqrt{9 + h}$ and $b = \sqrt{9}$

——

$\frac{1}{6}$

——

4-44 : What is $\lim\limits_{x \to 3} \dfrac{\sqrt{x} - \sqrt{3}}{x - 3}$? Use the identity of 4-43 with $a = \sqrt{x}$ and $b = \sqrt{3}$.

$$\frac{1}{\sqrt{3} + \sqrt{3}} = \frac{1}{2\sqrt{3}}$$

4-45 : What is $\lim\limits_{h \to 0} \dfrac{\sqrt[3]{9 + h} - \sqrt[3]{9}}{h}$? *Hint:*

$a^3 - b^3 = (a - b)(a^2 + ab + b^2)$

Let $a = \sqrt[3]{9 + h}$ and $b = \sqrt[3]{9}$.

$$\frac{1}{3\sqrt[3]{9^2}} \frac{\sqrt[3]{9 + h} - \sqrt[3]{9}}{h}$$

$$= \frac{\sqrt[3]{9 + h} - \sqrt[3]{9}}{h} \cdot \frac{\sqrt[3]{9 + h^2} + \sqrt[3]{9 + h}\,\sqrt[3]{9} + \sqrt[3]{9^2}}{\sqrt[3]{9 + h^2} + \sqrt[3]{9 + h}\,\sqrt[3]{9} + \sqrt[3]{9^2}}$$

$$= \frac{(9 + h) - 9}{h(\sqrt[3]{9 + h^2} + \sqrt[3]{9 + h}\,\sqrt[3]{9} + \sqrt[3]{9^2})}$$

$$= \frac{1}{\sqrt[3]{9 + h^2} - \sqrt[3]{9 + h}\,\sqrt[3]{9} + \sqrt[3]{9^2}}$$

Therefore

$$\lim\limits_{h \to 0} \frac{\sqrt[3]{9 + h} - \sqrt[3]{9}}{h} = \frac{1}{\sqrt[3]{9^2} + \sqrt[3]{9^2} + \sqrt[3]{9^2}} = \frac{1}{3\sqrt[3]{9^2}}$$

In the Problem Set in the back of this text, Probs. 51 to 55 are of this same type. The interested student may wish to do these problems now.

We now list a number of definitions for reference. The reader may cover different portions of each definition to see whether he would write that portion just as it is presented here, or skip them and go on to Chap. 5.

$\lim\limits_{x \to c} f(x) = L$ if and only if

    for each positive real number ε

    there exists a positive real number δ

        such that

    for each x in the domain of f

$$0 < |x - c| < \delta \Rightarrow |f(x) - L| < \varepsilon$$

$\lim\limits_{x \to 2} x^3 = 8$ if and only if

    for each positive real number ε

    there exists a positive real number δ

        such that

    for each x in the domain of $\{(x, x^3)\}$

$$0 < |x - 2| < \delta \Rightarrow |x^3 - 8| < \varepsilon$$

$\lim\limits_{x \to +\infty} f(x) = L$ if and only if

    for each positive real number ε

    there exists a positive real number N

        such that

    for each x in the domain of f

$$x > N \Rightarrow |f(x) - L| < \varepsilon$$

$\lim\limits_{x \to +\infty} 1/x = 0$ if and only if

    for each positive real number ε

    there exists a positive real number N

        such that

    for each x in the domain of $\{(x, 1/x)\}$

$$x > N \Rightarrow \left| \frac{1}{x} - 0 \right| < \varepsilon$$

$\lim_{x \to c} f(x) = +\infty$ if and only if

    for each positive real number M

    there exists a positive real number δ

        such that

    for each x in the domain of f

$$0 < |x - c| < \delta \Rightarrow f(x) > M$$

$\lim_{x \to 3} \dfrac{1}{x - 3} = +\infty$ if and only if

    for each positive real number M

    there exists a positive real number δ

        such that

    for each x in the domain of $\left\{ \left(x, \dfrac{1}{x - 3} \right) \right\}$

$$0 < |x - c| < \delta \Rightarrow \dfrac{1}{x - 3} > M$$

$\lim_{x \to +\infty} f(x) = +\infty$ if and only

    for each positive real number M

    there exists a positive real number N

        such that

    for each x in the domain of f

$$x > N < \delta \Rightarrow f(x) > M$$

$\lim_{x \to \infty} x^2 = +\infty$ if and only if

    for each positive real number M

    there exists a positive real number N

        such that

    for each x in the domain of $\{ (x, x^2) \}$

$$x > N \Rightarrow x^2 > M$$

$\lim\limits_{x \to -\infty} f(x) = +\infty$ **if and only if**

    for each positive real number M

    there exists a positive real number N

        such that

    for each x in the domain of f

$$x < -N \Rightarrow f(x) > M$$

$\lim\limits_{x \to -\infty} f(x) = -\infty$ **if and only if**

    for each positive real number M

    there exists a positive real number N

        such that

    for each x in the domain of f

$$x < -N \Rightarrow f(x) < -M$$

$\lim\limits_{x \to +\infty} f(x) = -\infty$ **if and only if**

    for each positive real number M

    there exists a positive real number N

        such that

    for each x in the domain of f

$$x > N \Rightarrow f(x) < -M$$

$\lim\limits_{x \to c+} f(x) = L$ **if and only if**

    for each positive real number ε

    there exists a positive real number δ

        such that

    for each x in the domain of f

$$0 < (x - c) < \delta \Rightarrow |f(x) - L| < \varepsilon$$

$\lim\limits_{x \to 0+} \dfrac{|x|}{x} = 1$ **if and only if**

for each positive real number ε
there exists a positive real number δ
  such that
for each x in the domain of $\{(x, |x|/x)\}$

$$0 < (x - 0) < \delta \Rightarrow \left| \frac{|x|}{x} - 1 \right| < \varepsilon$$

$\lim\limits_{x \to c-} f(x) = L$ **if and only if**

for each positive real number ε
there exists a positive real number δ
  such that
for each x in the domain of f

$$0 < (c - x) < \delta \Rightarrow |f(x) - L| < \varepsilon$$

$\lim\limits_{x \to 0-} \dfrac{|x|}{x} = -1$ **if and only if**

for each positive real number ε
there exists a positive real number δ
  such that
for each x in the domain of $\{(x, |x|/x)\}$

$$0 < (0 - x) < \delta \Rightarrow \left| \frac{|x|}{x} - (-1) \right| < \varepsilon$$

$\lim\limits_{x \to c+} f(x) = +\infty$ **if and only if**

for each positive real number M
there exists a positive real number δ

such that

for each x in the domain of f

$$0 < (x - c) < \delta \Rightarrow f(x) > M$$

$\lim\limits_{x \to 0+} \dfrac{1}{x} = +\infty$ if and only if

for each positive real number M

there exists a positive real number δ

such that

for each x in the domain of $\{(x, 1/x)\}$

$$0 < (x - 0) < \delta \Rightarrow \frac{1}{x} > M$$

$\lim\limits_{x \to 0-} \dfrac{1}{x} = -\infty$ if and only if

for each positive real number M

there exists a positive real number δ

such that

for each x in the domain of $\{(x, 1/x)\}$

$$0 < (0 - x) < \delta \Rightarrow \frac{1}{x} < -M$$

$\lim\limits_{x \to -\infty} x^2 = +\infty$ if and only if

for each positive real number M

there exists a positive real number N

such that

for each x in the domain of $\{(x, x^2)\}$

$$x < -N \Rightarrow x^2 > M$$

$\lim\limits_{x \to +\infty} x^2 = +\infty$ if and only if

for each positive real number M

there exists a positive real number N

such that

for each x in the domain of $\{(x, x^2)\}$

$x > N \Rightarrow x^2 > M$

$\lim\limits_{x \to -\infty} -x^2 = -\infty$ **if and only if**

for each positive real number M

there exists a positive real number N

    such that

for each x in the domain of $\{(x, -x^2)\}$

$x < -N \Rightarrow -x^2 < -M$

$\lim\limits_{x \to +\infty} -x^2 = -\infty$ **if and only if**

for each positive real number M

there exists a positive real number N

    such that

for each x in the domain of $\{(x, -x^2)\}$

$x > N \Rightarrow -x^2 < -M$

f is continuous at b in the domain of f if and only if

for each positive real number ε

there exists a positive real number δ

    such that

for each x in the domain of f

$|x - b| < \delta \Rightarrow |f(x) - f(b)| < \varepsilon$

The following four definitions are of functions defined on the domain of natural numbers (sequences):

$\lim\limits_{n \to \infty} f_n = L$ **if and only if**

for each positive real number ε

there exists a natural number N

    such that

$n \geq N \Rightarrow |f_n - L| < \varepsilon$

$\lim\limits_{n\to\infty} \dfrac{1}{2^n} = 0$ if and only if

for each positive real number ε
there exists a natural number N
such that

$$n \geq N \Rightarrow \left| \dfrac{1}{2^n} - 0 \right| < \varepsilon$$

$\lim\limits_{n\to\infty} \left(3 + \dfrac{(-1)^n}{n} \right) = 3$ if and only if

for each positive real number ε
there exists a natural number N
such that

$$n \geq N \Rightarrow \left| \left(3 + \dfrac{(-1)^n}{n} \right) - 3 \right| < \varepsilon$$

$\lim\limits_{n\to\infty} n^2 = \infty$ if and only if

for each positive real number M
there exists a natural number N
such that

$$n \geq N \Rightarrow n^2 > M$$

Chapter Five: Theorems on Continuity and Limits

In this chapter we shall state some theorems and definitions traditionally associated with the topic of limits and continuity. These theorems give the student something concrete to refer to as a reason for a given step in a proof or as a justification for a step in future problems.

DEFINITION 5-1:

$$f + g = \{(x, y)|y = f(x) + g(x),\ x \in D_f \cap D_g\}$$

The function $f + g$ is defined to be the set of all ordered pairs (x, y) such that y is the sum of the values of the functions f and g at x, where x is in both the domain of f and the domain of g.

If $f(x) = 3x - 1$ and $g(x) = 2x + 3$, then $(f + g)(x)$ is $(3x - 1) + (2x + 3) = 5x + 2$.

DEFINITION 5-2:

$$f - g = \{(x, y)|y = f(x) - g(x),\ x \in D_f \cap D_g\}$$

The function $f - g$ is defined to be the set of all ordered pairs (x, y) such that y is the difference of the values of f and g at x, where x is in both the domain of f and the domain of g.

If $f(x) = 3x - 1$ and $g(x) = 2x + 3$, then $(f - g)(x)$ is $(3x - 1) - (2x + 3) = x - 4$.

DEFINITION 5-3:

$$fg = \{(x, y)|y = f(x)g(x),\ x \in D_f \cap D_g\}$$

The function fg is defined to be the set of all (x, y) such that y is the product of the values of f and g at x, where x is in both the domain of f and the domain of g.

If $f(x) = 3x - 1$ and $g(x) = 2x + 3$, then $fg(x)$ is $(3x - 1)(2x + 3) = 6x^2 + 7x - 3$.

DEFINITION 5-4:

$$\frac{f}{g} = \left\{(x, y)|y = \frac{f(x)}{g(x)},\ g(x) \neq 0,\ x \in D_f \cap D_g\right\}$$

The function f/g is defined to be the set of all (x, y) such that y is the quotient of the values of f and g at x, $g(x)$ is not 0, and x is in both the domain of f and the domain of g.

DEFINITION 5-5:

$$f \circ g = \{(x, y)|y = f(g(x)),\ x \in D_g,\ g(x) \in D_f\}$$

The composite of two functions, $f \circ g$, is the set of all ordered pairs (x, y) such that y is in the range of f, the image of x under g is the preimage of y under f, and x is in the domain of g.

This can also be symbolized

$$f \circ g = \{(x, y)|(x, g(x)) \in g,\ (g(x), y) \in f\}$$

Figure 5-1 illustrates the composite $f \circ g$ where

$$f = \{(x, y)|y = 3x - 1\}$$

and $g = \{(x, y)|y = 2x + 3\}$. Under the first part of this composition g maps x onto $2x + 3$; then f completes the second part of the composition by mapping $2x + 3$ onto $3(2x + 3) - 1$. Under the first part of this composition, g maps 4 onto 11; then f maps 11 onto 32. Also, g maps 1 onto 5; then f maps 5 onto 14.

In Fig. 5-2 we illustrate the composite $g \circ f$. This time f maps x onto $3x - 1$; then g maps $3x - 1$ onto $2(3x - 1) + 3$. $g \circ f$ would map 4 onto 25. First f maps 4 onto 11; then g maps 11 onto 25. $g \circ f$ would map 1 onto 7. First f maps 1 onto 2; then g maps 2 onto 7.

$f \circ g(x)$ means first to find $g(x)$ and then to find f of $g(x)$; that is, $f \circ g(x) = f(g(x))$.

We shall now state and prove several theorems. The first few theorems prove the following statement.

If f and g are continuous at b, then

A: $f + g$ is continuous at b.

B: $f - g$ is continuous at b.

C: fg is continuous at b.

D: f/g is continuous at b, provided $g(b) \neq 0$.

E: $f \circ g$ is continuous at b, provided that $g(b) \in D_f$ and that f is continuous at $g(b)$.

Figure 5-1

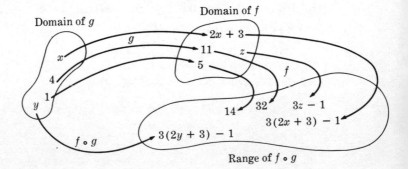

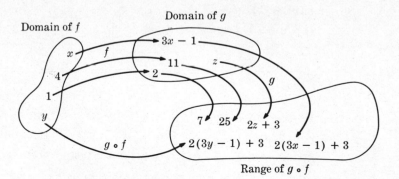

Figure 5-2

We shall use the following two definitions throughout the proofs, so we shall state them here and then refer to them as $D1$ and $D2$.

D1:

f is continuous at b if and only if
  for each positive real number ε_1
  there exists a positive real number δ_1
    such that
  for each x in the domain of *f*

$$|x - b| < \delta_1 \Rightarrow |f(x) - f(b)| < \varepsilon_1$$

D2:

g is continuous at b if and only if
  for each positive real number ε_2
  there exists a positive real number δ_2
    such that
  for each x in the domain of *g*

$$|x - b| < \delta_2 \Rightarrow |g(x) - g(b)| < \varepsilon_2$$

THEOREM 5-1:

If f and g are continuous at b, then f + g is continuous at b.

Proof:

1: For any given ε, take $\varepsilon_1 = \varepsilon_2 = \varepsilon/2$. From *D*1 and *D*2,

2: There exist δ_1 and δ_2 satisfying *D*1 and *D*2.

3: Choose $\delta = \min\{\delta_1, \delta_2\}$. This choice of δ ensures us that if

4: $|x - b| < \delta$

then

5: $|f(x) - f(b)| < \varepsilon_1 = \dfrac{\varepsilon}{2} \qquad |g(x) - g(b)| < \varepsilon_2 = \dfrac{\varepsilon}{2}$

Adding these expressions gives

6: $|f(x) - f(b)| + |g(x) - g(b)| < \dfrac{\varepsilon}{2} + \dfrac{\varepsilon}{2} = \varepsilon$

However

7: $|f(x) - f(b) + g(x) - g(b)| \leq |f(x) - f(b)| + |g(x) - g(b)|$

from which we conclude that

8: $|[f(x) + g(x)] - [f(b) + g(b)]| < \varepsilon$

or

$|(f + g)(x) - (f + g)(b)| < \varepsilon$

9: Therefore if $|x - b| < \delta$, then

$|(f + g)(x) - (f + g)(b)| < \varepsilon$

This is precisely the condition that $f + g$ be continuous at b.

THEOREM 5-2:

If g is continuous at b, then $-g$ is continuous at b.

Proof:

1: For any given ε, take $\varepsilon_2 = \varepsilon$ and $\delta = \delta_2$. If

2: $|x - b| < \delta$

then

3: $|g(x) - g(b)| < \varepsilon_2 = \varepsilon$

But from the properties of absolute value,

4: $|g(x) - g(b)| = |[-g(x)] - [-g(b)]|$

so that

5: $|[-g(x)] - [-g(b)]| < \varepsilon$

which proves that $-g$ is continuous at b.

THEOREM 5-3:

If f and g are continuous at b, then $f - g$ is continuous at b.

Proof:

By Theorems 5-1 and 5-2,

1: $f + (-g)$ is continuous at b.

But since $f + (-g) = f - g$,

2: $f - g$ is continuous at b.

THEOREM 5-4:

If f and g are continuous at b, then fg is continuous at b.

Proof:

1: For a given ε, take $\varepsilon_1, \varepsilon_2 > 0$ such that

$$\varepsilon_1\varepsilon_2 + |g(b)|\varepsilon_1 + |f(b)|\varepsilon_2 < \varepsilon$$

This is easily done by making ε_1 and ε_2 small enough so that $\varepsilon_1\varepsilon_2 < \varepsilon/3$, $|g(b)|\varepsilon_1 < \varepsilon/3$, and $|f(b)|\varepsilon_2 < \varepsilon/3$. It should be remarked that the choice of ε_1 and ε_2 is not the result of some mystic insight of the problem but is determined by working the steps of the proof backward from the desired result in order to determine what is needed.

2: Choose $\delta = \min\{\delta_1, \delta_2\}$.   If

3: $|x - b| < \delta$

then

4: $|f(x) - f(b)| < \varepsilon_1$ $|g(x) - g(b)| < \varepsilon_2$

Multiplying these two expressions gives

5: $|f(x)g(x) - f(b)g(x) - g(b)f(x) + f(b)g(b)| < \varepsilon_1\varepsilon_2$

We should like the left-hand side of 5 to be $|f(x)g(x) - f(b)g(b)|$. Accordingly, we add $|f(b)g(x) + g(b)f(x) - 2f(b)g(b)|$ to both sides of 5 and apply the general result $|x + y| \leq |x| + |y|$ on the left.

6: $|f(x)g(x) - f(b)g(b)|$
$< \varepsilon_1\varepsilon_2 + |f(b)g(x) + g(b)f(x) - 2f(b)g(b)|$

7: $\leq \varepsilon_1\varepsilon_2 + |f(b)|\,|g(x) - g(b)| + |g(b)|\,|f(x) - f(b)|$

8: $< \varepsilon_1\varepsilon_2 + |f(b)|\varepsilon_2 + |g(b)|\varepsilon_1$

9: $< \varepsilon$

10: Therefore, if $|x - b| < \delta$, then $|fg(x) - fg(b)| < \varepsilon$. This shows that fg is continuous at b.

THEOREM 5-5:

If g is continuous at b and $g(b) \neq 0$, then $1/g$ is continuous at b.

Before we start the formal proof, we shall establish some symbolism.

If we are given $\varepsilon' = \frac{1}{3}|g(b)|$, then by $D2$ there exists a δ' such that

$$|x - b| < \delta' \Rightarrow |g(x) - g(b)| < \varepsilon'$$

so

A: $\quad |g(x) - g(b)| < \frac{1}{3}|g(b)|$

B: $\quad |g(b) - g(x)| < \frac{1}{3}|g(b)|$

C: $\quad |g(b)| - |g(x)| < \frac{1}{3}|g(b)|$

D: $\quad -|g(b)| + |g(x)| > -\frac{1}{3}|g(b)|$

E: $\quad |g(x)| > \frac{2}{3}|g(b)|$

and

F: $\quad \dfrac{1}{|g(x)|} < \dfrac{3}{2}\dfrac{1}{|g(b)|}$

Proof:

1: For any given ε, take $\varepsilon'' = \frac{2}{3}|g(b)|^2$; then there is a δ'' such that $|x - b| < \delta'' \rightarrow |g(x) - g(b)| < \varepsilon''$.

2: Choose $\delta = \min\{\delta', \delta''\}$. If

3: $\quad |x - b| < \delta$

then

4: $\quad |g(x) - g(b)| < \varepsilon''$

If we multiply (4) by

F: $\quad \dfrac{1}{|g(x)|} < \dfrac{3}{2}\dfrac{1}{|g(b)|}$

we get

5: $\quad \dfrac{|g(x) - g(b)|}{|g(x)|} < \dfrac{3}{2|g(b)|}\,\varepsilon''$

Multiplying each side by $1/|g(b)|$ gives

6: $\quad \dfrac{|g(x) - g(b)|}{|g(x)g(b)|} < \dfrac{3}{2|g(b)|^2}\,\varepsilon''$

7: $\left| \dfrac{1}{g(b)} - \dfrac{1}{g(x)} \right| < \dfrac{3}{2|g(b)|^2} \dfrac{2}{3} |g(b)|^2 \varepsilon$

8: $\left| \dfrac{1}{g(x)} - \dfrac{1}{g(b)} \right| < \varepsilon$

Therefore

9: $|x - b| < \delta \Rightarrow \left| \dfrac{1}{g(x)} - \dfrac{1}{g(b)} \right| < \varepsilon$

This shows that $1/g$ is continuous at b.

THEOREM 5-6:

If f and g are continuous at b and $g(b) \neq 0$, then f/g is continuous at b.

Proof:

$f/g = (f)(1/g)$ and since Theorem 5-5 shows that $1/g$ is continuous at b, we have that f/g is continuous at b by Theorem 5-4.

THEOREM 5-7:

If the function g is continuous at b and the function f is continuous at $g(b)$, then the composite $f \circ g$ is continuous at b.

If f is continuous at $g(b)$, then

A: for each positive real number ε_1

there exists a positive real number δ_1

such that

for each $g(x)$ in the domain of f

$|g(x) - g(b)| < \delta_1 \Rightarrow |f(g(x)) - f(g(b))| < \varepsilon_1$

g is continuous at b if and only if

B: for each positive real number ε_2
there exists a positive real number δ_2
such that
for each x in the domain of g

$$|x - b| < \delta_2 \Rightarrow |g(x) - g(b)| < \varepsilon_2$$

Proof:

1:   For any given ε, let $\varepsilon_1 = \varepsilon$, and $\varepsilon_2 = \delta_1$.   If
2: $|x - b| < \delta_2$
then
3: $|g(x) - g(b)| < \varepsilon_2$
But $\varepsilon_2 = \delta_1$, so by A
4: $|f(g(x)) - f(g(b))| < \varepsilon_1$
Therefore,
5: $|x - b| < \delta_2 \Rightarrow |f(g(x)) - f(g(b))| < \varepsilon$

This is precisely the statement that $f \circ g$ is continuous at b.

THEOREM 5-8:
The constant function $k = \{(x,y)|y = c, \text{where } c \text{ is a constant}\}$
is continuous at all points b of its domain.

Proof:
Since $|k(x) - k(b)| = |c - c| = 0$ and $\varepsilon > 0$, we may conclude that $|k(x) - k(b)| < \varepsilon$ regardless of the δ we choose. Therefore, k is continuous at all points b in its domain.

THEOREM 5-9:
The identity function $I = \{(x, y)|y = x\}$ *is continuous at all points of its domain.*

Proof:

Since $|I(x) - I(b)| = |x - b|$, it is immediate that for any $\delta \leq \varepsilon, |x - b| < \delta \Rightarrow |x - b| < \varepsilon$. Therefore, the identity function is continuous at all points b in its domain.

DEFINITION 5-6:

A function P is a *polynomial function* if and only if it may be defined by an expression of the form

$$P(x) = b_0 x^n + b_1 x^{n-1} + \cdots + b_{n-3} x^3 + b_{n-2} x^2 \\ + b_{n-1} x + b_n$$

where n is a positive integer and $b_0, b_1, \ldots, b_{n-1}$, b_n are real numbers.

THEOREM 5-10:

Any polynomial function is continuous at b for any real number b.

Proof:

Let $P(x)$ define any polynomial function. Recall from Theorems 5-8 and 5-9 that the functions defined by $k(x) = c$ and $I(x) = x$ are continuous at b. By repeated applications of Theorem 5-4, cx^p defines a function continuous at b for any constant c and any positive integer p. Thus each of the terms of $P(x)$ defines a function continuous at b. By repeated applications of Theorem 5-1, P is continuous at b.

DEFINITION 5-7:

A function R is a *rational function* if and only if $R = P/Q$ for some polynomial functions P and Q.

THEOREM 5-11:

A rational function $R = P/Q$ is continuous at any point b for which $Q(b) \neq 0$.

Proof:

By Theorem 5-10, P and Q are continuous at b. Therefore, if $Q(b) \neq 0$, then R is continuous at b by Theorem 5-6.

THEOREM 5-12:

Let b be a limit point of the domain of f. The following statements are equivalent to "f is continuous at the point b in the domain of f":

i) *for each positive real number ε*
there exists a positive real number δ
       such that
for each x in the domain of f
$$|x - b| < \delta \Rightarrow |f(x) - f(b)| < \varepsilon$$

ii) *for each positive real number ε*
there exists a positive real number δ
such that
$$\{(x, y) \in f|\ |x - b| < \delta\} \subseteq \{(x, y)|\ |x - b| < \delta,$$
$$|y - f(b)| < \varepsilon\}$$

iii) $\lim\limits_{x \to b} f(x) = f(b)$

iv) $\lim\limits_{h \to 0} f(b + h) = f(b)$

Proof:

By definition, (i) is equivalent to the statement that f is continuous at b. Then it is sufficient to prove that (i) implies (ii), (ii) implies (iii), (iii) implies (iv), and (iv) implies (i).

Proof that $(i) \Rightarrow (ii)$**:** (i) is the statement that for each $\varepsilon > 0$, there exists a $\delta > 0$ such that for each x in the domain of f, $|x - b| < \delta$ implies that $|f(x) - f(b)| < \varepsilon$. Let us write $A = \{(x, y) \in f |\ |x - b| < \delta\}$ and

$$B = \{(x, y)|\ |x - b| < \delta, |y - f(b)| < \varepsilon\}$$

We must prove that, given any $\varepsilon > 0$, there is a $\delta > 0$ such that $A \subseteq B$, in other words, that (for this ε and δ) $(x, f(x)) \in A \Rightarrow (x, f(x)) \in B$. For each ε, we choose the δ used in (i). If $(x, f(x)) \in A$, then $|x - b| < \delta$. From (i), it follows that $|f(x) - f(b)| < \varepsilon$. But then $(x, f(x))$ satisfies the conditions for membership in B, so that $(x, f(x)) \in B$. Hence, (i) implies (ii).

Proof that $(ii) \Rightarrow (iii)$**:** For each $\varepsilon > 0$, choose $\delta > 0$ as given by (ii). Then for each x in the domain of f, if $|x - b| < \delta$, that is, if $(x, f(x)) \in A$, then $(x, f(x)) \in B$, which says that $|f(x) - f(b)| < \varepsilon$. Since this is true for every x in the domain of f such that $|x - b| < \delta$, it must still be true for every x in the domain of f satisfying the conditions that $|x - b| > 0$ and $|x - b| < \delta$. So we have

   for each positive real number ε

   there exists a positive real number δ

      such that

   for each x in the domain of f

$$0 < |x - b| < \delta \Rightarrow |f(x) - f(b)| < \varepsilon$$

which, since b is a limit point of the domain of f, is defined as the statement $\lim_{x \to b} f(x) = f(b)$. Hence, (ii) implies (iii).

Proof that $(iii) \Rightarrow (iv)$**:** If we replace x with $b + h$ everywhere in the definition of $\lim_{x \to b} f(x) = f(b)$, we obtain for each positive real number ε

there exists a positive real number δ

    such that

for each $b + h$ in the domain of f

$$0 < |h - 0| < \delta \Rightarrow |f(b + h) - f(b)| < \varepsilon$$

which is the statement that $\lim\limits_{h \to 0} f(b + h) = f(b)$. There-fore, (iii) implies (iv).

Proof that $(iv) \Rightarrow (i)$: If, in the above definition of $\lim\limits_{h \to 0} f(b + h) = f(b)$, we are to remove the restriction that $|h - 0|$ be unequal to 0, we must show that

$$|h - 0| = 0 \Rightarrow |f(b + h) - f(b)| < \varepsilon$$

$|h - 0| = 0$ only if $h = 0$. In this case,

$$f(b + h) = f(b + 0) = f(b)$$

whence $|f(b + h) - f(b)| = |f(b) - f(b)| = 0$, which is less than any ε, since $\varepsilon > 0$. Therefore, we write

for each positive real number ε

there exists a positive real number δ

    such that

for each $b + h$ in the domain of f

$$|h - 0| < \delta \Rightarrow |f(b + h) - f(b)| < \varepsilon$$

If we replace h with $x - b$, this becomes

for each positive real number ε

there exists a positive real number δ

    such that

for each x in the domain of f

$$|x - b| < \delta \Rightarrow |f(x) - f(b)| < \varepsilon$$

This shows that (iv) implies (i) and completes the proof.

THEOREM 5-13:
If $\lim\limits_{x \to b} f(x) = L_1$ *and* $\lim\limits_{x \to b} f(x) = L_2$, *then* $L_1 = L_2$.

By hypothesis we have

for each positive real number ε_1
there exists a positive real number δ_1
    such that
for each x in the domain of f

A: $0 < |x - b| < \delta_1 \Rightarrow |f(x) - L_1| < \varepsilon_1$

and

for each positive real number ε_2
there exists a positive real number δ_2
    such that
for each x in the domain of f

B: $0 < |x - b| < \delta_2 \Rightarrow |f(x) - L_2| < \varepsilon_2$

Proof:

1: Suppose that $L_1 \neq L_2$. Then L_1 and L_2 have a distance $\varepsilon > 0$ between them; that is,

2: $L_1 - L_2 = \varepsilon$

In reference to A and B, take

3: $\varepsilon_1 = \varepsilon_2 = \dfrac{\varepsilon}{3}$ and $\delta = \min \{\delta_1, \delta_2\}$

If

4: $0 < |x - b| < \delta$

then

5: $|f(x) - L_1| < \dfrac{\varepsilon}{3} \qquad |f(x) - L_2| < \dfrac{\varepsilon}{3}$

From this,

6: $|f(x) - L_1| + |f(x) - L_2| < \dfrac{\varepsilon}{3} + \dfrac{\varepsilon}{3}$

7: $|L_1 - f(x)| + |f(x) - L_2| < \dfrac{2\varepsilon}{3}$

8: $|L_1 - f(x) + f(x) - L_2| < \dfrac{2\varepsilon}{3}$

9: $|L_1 - L_2| < \dfrac{2\varepsilon}{3}$

But we started the proof by assuming that

10: $|L_1 - L_2| = \varepsilon$

This implies that $\varepsilon < 2\varepsilon/3$ and $3\varepsilon < 2\varepsilon$, which is absurd since $\varepsilon > 0$. Therefore, our assumption that $L_1 \neq L_2$ is untenable, and we must conclude that $L_1 = L_2$.

THEOREM 5-14:

If $\lim\limits_{x \to b} f(x) = L_1$ *and* $\lim\limits_{x \to b} g(x) = L_2$, *then*

i) $\lim\limits_{x \to b} (f + g)(x) = L_1 + L_2$

ii) $\lim\limits_{x \to b} (f - g)(x) = L_1 - L_2$

iii) $\lim_{x \to b} (fg)(x) = L_1 L_2$

iv) $\lim_{x \to b} \left(\dfrac{f}{g}\right)(x) = \dfrac{L_1}{L_2}$ *provided $L_2 \neq 0$*

The steps followed in the proof of this theorem are practically identical with those followed in the proofs of the complementary theorems on continuity, so we shall not give the proof here.

In the next theorem the notation $(a; c)$ is used to symbolize the open interval $\{x | a < x < c\}$. If this notation is new, you may wish to read that portion of the Appendix which covers it.

THEOREM 5-15:
Suppose $f(x) \leq g(x) \leq h(x)$ for all $x \in (a; c)$, except perhaps at $x = b \in (a; c)$. If $\lim_{x \to b} f(x) = \lim_{x \to b} h(x) = L$, then
$\lim_{x \to b} g(x) = L.$

We are given that for each $\varepsilon_1 > 0$ and $\varepsilon_2 > 0$, there are $\delta_1 > 0$ and $\delta_2 > 0$ such that for each x in the domain of f and h

A: $0 < |x - b| < \delta_1 \Rightarrow |f(x) - L| < \varepsilon_1$
B: $0 < |x - b| < \delta_2 \Rightarrow |h(x) - L| < \varepsilon_2$

We must show that

for each positive real number ε
there exists a positive real number δ
    such that

for each x in the domain of g

$0 < |x - b| < \delta \Rightarrow |g(x) - L| < \varepsilon$

Proof:

1: For any ε, let $\varepsilon_1 = \varepsilon_2 = \varepsilon$ and

$\delta = \min \{\delta_1, \delta_2, |b - a|, |b - c|\}$

If

2: $0 < |x - b| < \delta$

then

3: $|f(x) - L| < \varepsilon$ or $L - \varepsilon < f(x) < L + \varepsilon$

and

$|h(x) - L| < \varepsilon$ or $L - \varepsilon < h(x) < L + \varepsilon$

and

4: $f(x) \leq g(x) \leq h(x)$

Combining these gives

5: $L - \varepsilon < f(x) \leq g(x) \leq h(x) < L + \varepsilon$

6: $L - \varepsilon < g(x) < L + \varepsilon$

which is equivalent to

7: $|g(x) - L| < \varepsilon$

Therefore,

$\lim\limits_{x \to b} g(x) = L$

It is sometimes practical to use the rule, "the limit of the function is the function of the limit." If we are asked to find $\lim\limits_{x \to 4} (x + 1)^3$, we can use this rule as follows:

$$\lim_{x \to 4} (x + 1)^3 = (\lim_{x \to 4} (x + 1))^3 = 5^3 = 125$$

In this example (Fig. 5-3) we are finding the limit of the composition of two functions. Let $f = \{(x, y) | y = x^3\}$ and $g = \{(x, y) | y = x + 1\}$; then $f \circ g = \{(x, y) | y = (x + 1)^3\}$. So, when we let

$$\lim_{x \to 4} (x + 1)^3 = (\lim_{x \to 4} (x + 1))^3$$

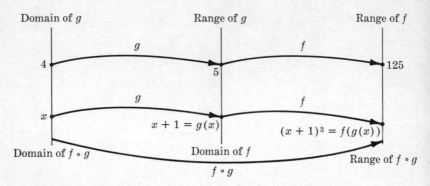

Figure 5-3

we are using the fact that

$$\lim_{x \to b} (f \circ g)(x) = f(\lim_{x \to b} g(x))$$

This rule is correct most of the time in the study of calculus, but we are interested in the few times it is not correct. It is used correctly in the following discussion of Fig. 5-4.

$$\lim_{x \to 100} (\log x^2) = \log (\lim_{x \to 100} x^2) = \log 10,000 = 4$$

If we let $f = \{(x, y)|y = \log x\}$ and $g = \{(x, y)|y = x^2\}$, then $f \circ g = \{(x, y)|y = \log x^2\}$; so when we let

$$\lim_{x \to 100} (\log x^2) = \log (\lim_{x \to 100} x^2)$$

we are using the fact that

$$\lim_{x \to b} (f \circ g)(x) = f(\lim_{x \to b} g(x))$$

On the other hand in Fig. 5-5 if we let $g = \{(x, y)|y = x\}$ and $f = \{(x, y)|y = 1$ when $x \neq 0, y = 2$ when $x = 0\}$, our

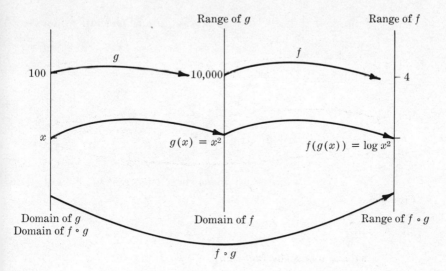

Figure 5-4

Figure 5-5

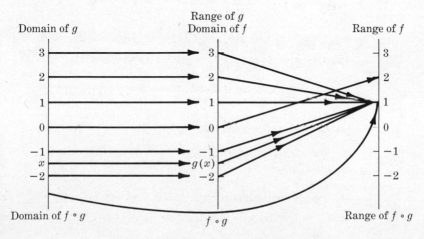

"limit of the function is the function of the limit" does not work, as

$$\lim_{x \to 0} (f \circ g)(x) = \lim_{x \to 0} f(g(x)) = 1$$

whereas

$$f(\lim_{x \to 0} g(x)) = f(0) = 2$$

We now state and prove three theorems which will show when

$$\lim_{x \to b} (f \circ g)(x) = f(\lim_{x \to b} g(x))$$

is applicable. In the first theorem we shall assume both that f is continuous at $g(b)$ and g is continuous at b. In the second we shall not insist that g be continuous at b, but we will insist that g have a limit at b. In the third theorem we insist that g have a limit at b and f have a limit at $f(b)$.

THEOREM 5-16:

If f and g are functions such that
g is continuous at a point b,
f is continuous at a point $g(b)$,
and b is a limit point of the domain of $f \circ g$, then

$$\lim_{x \to b} (f \circ g)(x) = f(\lim_{x \to b} g(x))$$

Proof:

1: g is continuous at b.
   f is continuous at $f(b)$.
   By Theorem 5-7

2: $f \circ g$ is continuous at b.

Therefore, by (iii) of Theorem 5-12

3: $\lim_{x \to b} (f \circ g)(x) = (f \circ g)(b)$

By definition of composition

4: $\lim_{x \to b} (f \circ g)(x) = f(g(b))$

but since g is continuous, by (iii) of Theorem 5-12

5: $\lim_{x \to b} (f \circ g)(x) = f(\lim_{x \to b} g(x))$

Now we change the hypothesis slightly by insisting that g have a limit at b rather than retaining the more stringent restriction that g be continuous at b.

THEOREM 5-17, Fig. 5-6:

If f and g are functions such that

$\lim_{x \to b} g(x) = c,$

f is continuous at c,

Figure 5-6

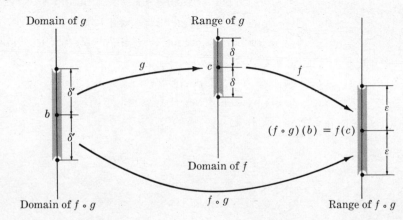

and b is a limit point of the domain of f ∘ g, then

$$\lim_{x \to b} (f \circ g)(x) = f(\lim_{x \to b} g(x))$$

Proof:

Since f is continuous at c,

1: for each positive real number ε

there exists a positive real number δ

such that

for each y in the domain of f

$$|y - c| < \delta \to |f(y) - f(c)| < \varepsilon$$

Since $\lim_{x \to b} g(x) = c$,

2: for each positive real number δ

there exists a positive real number δ'

such that

for each x in the domain of g

$$0 < |x - b| < \delta' \Rightarrow |g(x) - c| < \delta$$

But the y in statement 1 is the $g(x)$ in statement 2; therefore by substituting $g(x)$ for y in statement 1

3: $|g(x) - c| < \delta \Rightarrow |f(g(x)) - f(c)| < \varepsilon$

Then, for each x which is a limit point of the domain of $f \circ g$

4: $0 < |x - b| < \delta' \Rightarrow |f(g(x)) - f(c)| < \varepsilon$

This is by definition the statement that

5: $\lim_{x \to b} (f \circ g)(x) - f(c)$

but

6: $c = \lim_{x \to b} g(x)$

so

7: $f(c) = f(\lim_{x \to b} g(x))$

From 5 and 7

8: $\lim_{x \to b} (f \circ g)(x) = f(\lim_{x \to b} g(x))$

In the next theorem we insist only that f and g have a limit at the appropriate points. We shall not require that either be continuous at the point in question.

THEOREM 5-18:

If f and g are functions such that

A: $\lim_{x \to b} g(x) = c$

B: $\lim_{y \to c} f(y) = d$

C: *there exists a positive real number δ'*

such that

for each x in the domain of $f \circ g$

$$0 < |x - b| < \delta' \Rightarrow 0 < |g(x) - c|$$

and if b is a limit point of the domain of $f \circ g$, then

$$\lim_{x \to b} (f \circ g)(x) = \lim_{y \to c} f(y)$$

Proof:

1: Statement B assures us that

for each positive real number ε

there exists a positive real number δ

such that

for each y in the domain of f

$$0 < |y - c| < \delta \Rightarrow |f(y) - d| < \varepsilon$$

2: Statement A assures us that

for each positive real number δ

there exists a positive real number δ''

    such that

for each x in the domain of g

$$0 < |x - b| < \delta'' \Rightarrow |g(x) - c| < \delta$$

If we choose $\delta = \min \{\delta', \delta''\}$ and substitute the $g(x)$ from 2 for y in 1, we have

3: $\quad 0 < |g(x) - c| < \delta \Rightarrow |f(g(x)) - d| < \varepsilon$

But since C assures us that $0 < |g(x) - c|$, we have

4: $\quad 0 < |x - b| < \delta \Rightarrow |f(g(x)) - d| < \varepsilon$

This is the statement that

5: $\quad \lim\limits_{x \to b} f(g(x)) = d$

But, by B, $\lim\limits_{y \to c} f(y) = d$.   Therefore

6: $\quad \lim\limits_{x \to b} (f \circ g)(x) = \lim\limits_{z \to c} f(y)$

As an example of two functions that do not fit the hypotheses of Theorem 5-16 or 5-17 but do fit the hypotheses of Theorem 5-18, let $g = \{(x, y) | y = (x^2 - 4)/(x - 2)\}$ and let $f = \{(x, y) | y = (x^2 - 16)/(x - 4)\}$.   If we wish to find $\lim\limits_{x \to 2} (f \circ g)(x)$, we cannot use Theorem 5-16 or 5-17 since g is not continuous at 2 and f is not continuous at $g(2)$. In fact, g is not defined at 2.   However, 2 is a limit point of the domain of $f \circ g$,

$$\lim\limits_{x \to 2} g(x) = 4$$

$$\lim\limits_{y \to 4} f(y) = 6$$

and if $\delta' = 1$, then

$$0 < |x - 2| < \delta' \Rightarrow 0 < |g(x) - 4|$$

So we have all the hypotheses of Theorem 5-18.   Therefore,

$$\lim_{x \to 2} (f \circ g)(x) = \lim_{y \to 4} f(y) = 6$$

The surprising thing about this example is that 2 is not in the domain of g or in the domain of $f \circ g$, and 4 is not in the domain of f.   However, 2 is a limit point of the domain of g and of the domain of $f \circ g$, and 4 is a limit point of the domain of f.

Actually, we would not need nearly so many theorems in the calculus if all the points we discussed were in the domain and at the same time were limit points of the domain of the function we were discussing.

Throughout this book we have deliberately avoided discussing isolated points in the domain of a function, since there is some disagreement as to whether a function should be continuous at such points.   We discuss this problem now, using the following functions to show the differences between several definitions of continuity.   Let

$$f = \{(x, y)|y = \sqrt{x} \quad \text{when } x \geq 0\}$$

$$g = \{(x, y)|y = -1 \quad \text{when } x < -1$$
$$y = 0 \quad \text{when } x = 0$$
$$y = 1 \quad \text{when } x \geq 1\}$$

$$h = \{(x, y)|y = 1 \quad \text{when } x \text{ is rational}$$
$$y = -1 \quad \text{when } x \text{ is irrational}\}$$

$$k = \{(x, y)|y = 1 \quad \text{when } x \text{ is rational}\}$$

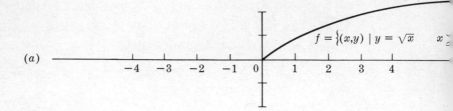

(a)

$f = \left\{(x,y) \mid y = \sqrt{x} \quad x \geq \right.$

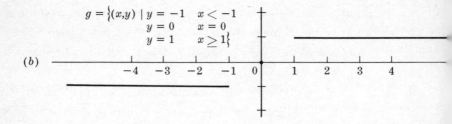

$g = \left\{(x,y) \mid \begin{array}{ll} y = -1 & x < -1 \\ y = 0 & x = 0 \\ y = 1 & x \geq 1 \end{array}\right\}$

(b)

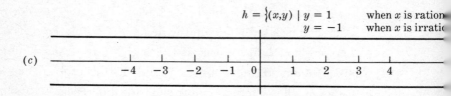

$h = \left\{(x,y) \mid \begin{array}{ll} y = 1 & \text{when } x \text{ is ration} \\ y = -1 & \text{when } x \text{ is irrati} \end{array}\right.$

(c)

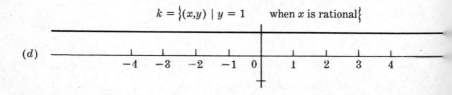

$k = \left\{(x,y) \mid y = 1 \quad \text{when } x \text{ is rational}\right\}$

(d)

Figure 5-7

We have graphed these functions in Fig. 5-7, and it may be helpful to look at them from time to time throughout the next discussion. Of course it is impossible for us to graph h and k accurately, since we cannot draw a line which represents only the rational points.

Some authors restrict continuity at a point to points which are limit points in the domain of the function in question. Nearly all definitions which define continuity in terms of the limit are of this type.

ALTERNATIVE DEFINITION A:

f is continuous at a limit point b in its domain if and only if
    for each positive real number ε
    there exists a positive real number δ
        such that
    for each x in the domain of f

$$|x - b| < \delta \Rightarrow |f(x) - f(b)| < \varepsilon$$

This definition will agree with our definition of continuity when applied to the functions in Fig. 5-7 except at 0 in function g. No isolated points of the domain can even be considered as substitutions for b by this definition, since they are not limit points of the domain of the function. Since our definition insists only that a point b be in the domain, we consider all isolated points of the domain to be points where the function is continuous. Since we demand that the only points x in $|x - 0| < \delta$ be points of the domain, the only point we consider in any neighborhood of 0 whose radius is less than 1 is 0 itself. The point 0 maps into $g(0)$, so by our definition g is continuous at 0.

The next definition we state demands that f be defined on some open interval that contains b or that has b as an end point. This definition disagrees with our definition not only at 0 in the function g but also at every point in the domain of k, since k is not defined on any interval.

ALTERNATIVE DEFINITION B:

Let f be defined on some open interval containing the point b or having b as an end point. The function f is continuous at b in its domain if and only if

 for each positive real number ε

 there exists a positive real number δ

  such that

 for each x in the domain of f

$$|x - b| < \delta \Rightarrow |f(x) - f(b)| < \varepsilon$$

Some authors say only that f must be defined on some open interval and do not allow b to be an end point of this interval. If this is done, then this definition will disagree with our definition at 0 in function f, at 0 and 1 in function g, and at every point in the domain of k.

We close this chapter by restating our definition of continuity at a point in the domain of a function.

f is continuous at a point b in the domain of f if and only if

 for each positive real number ε

 there exists a positive real number δ

  such that

 for each x in the domain of f

$$|x - b| < \delta \Rightarrow |f(x) - f(b)| < \varepsilon$$

Chapter Six: Preview of the Calculus

In this chapter we shall define the two main results of the study of limits and continuity. The differential and integral calculus are based historically upon the limit. We shall first define the integral and derivative in the traditional manner, using the concept of limit as a basis, then we shall define them in a new way, using continuity as a basis.

Before we do this, we investigate the process of summation. The next programmed exercise is designed to establish a notation for summation which will make defining an integral much easier.

6-1: The summation of five numbers can be written

$$\sum_{n=1}^{5} a_n = a_1 + a_2 + a_3 + a_4 + a_5$$

Examples:

$$\sum_{n=1}^{5} n = 1 + 2 + 3 + 4 + 5 = 15$$

$$\sum_{n=1}^{5} n^2 = 1 + 4 + 9 + 16 + 25 = 55$$

$$\sum_{n=1}^{5} \frac{1}{n} = \frac{1}{1} + \frac{1}{2} + \frac{1}{3} + \frac{1}{4} + \frac{1}{5} = \frac{137}{60}$$

Write out $\displaystyle\sum_{n=1}^{5} \frac{1}{n^2}$. Do not take time to add up the sum.

$\frac{1}{1} + \frac{1}{4} + \frac{1}{9} + \frac{1}{16} + \frac{1}{25}$

6-2 : The symbol $\displaystyle\sum_{n=1}^{5} a_n$ is read "the summation of a_n from $n = 1$ to 5." The summation of n^2 from $n = 1$ to 4 is

$$\sum_{n=1}^{4} n^2 = 1^2 + 2^2 + 3^2 + 4^2 = 30$$

What is the summation of n^2 from $n = 1$ to 3?

$n^2 = 1^2 + 2^2 + 3^2 = 14$

6-3 : All summations in this study are indexed on the natural numbers or nonnegative integers. The index of $\displaystyle\sum_{n=1}^{3} a_n$ is symbolized by n. We say that n is the index of the sum. In $\displaystyle\sum_{n=1}^{6} a_n$, the index runs from 1 to _____.

6

6-4 : The summation of $(n + 1)/n$ from $n = 1$ to 3 is

$$\sum_{n=1}^{3} \frac{n+1}{n} = \frac{1+1}{1} + \frac{2+1}{2} + \frac{3+1}{3}$$
$$= 2 + \frac{3}{2} + \frac{4}{3} = \frac{29}{6}$$

What is the summation of $(n^2 + 1)/n$ from $n = 1$ to 3?

$$\sum_{n=1}^{3} \frac{n^2+1}{n} = \frac{1^2+1}{1} + \frac{2^2+1}{2} + \frac{3^2+1}{3} = 2 + \frac{5}{2} + \frac{10}{3} = \frac{47}{6}$$

6-5 : The symbolism $\sum\limits_{n=1}^{\infty} a_n$ is read "the summation from 1 to infinity of a_n." The summation of $1/2^n$ from 1 to infinity is symbolized

$$\sum_{n=1}^{\infty} \frac{1}{2^n} = \frac{1}{2} + \frac{1}{4} + \frac{1}{8} + \cdots + \frac{1}{2^n} + \cdots = 1$$

This is the same sum with which Achilles had so much trouble in Chap. 2. This sum is called the sum of the sequence $(1/2^n)$. What is the sum of the sequence $(1/2^{n-1})$?

$$\sum_{n=1}^{\infty} \frac{1}{2^{n-1}} = \frac{1}{1} + \frac{1}{2} + \frac{1}{4} + \cdots + \frac{1}{2^{n-1}} + \cdots = 2$$

We know that this sum is 2 because it is equal to $1 + \sum\limits_{n=1}^{\infty} \dfrac{1}{2^n} = 2$.

6-6 : Any letter may be used for the index of a summation.

Example:

$$\sum_{k=1}^{n} k^3 = \sum_{p=1}^{n} p^3 = \sum_{t=1}^{n} t^3$$

All represent $1^3 + 2^3 + 3^3 + \cdots + n^3$.

Write the summation notation for $2^1 + 2^2 + 2^3 + 2^4 + \cdots + 2^n$ with several indices.

$$\sum_{k=1}^{n} 2^k = \sum_{\alpha=1}^{n} 2^\alpha = \sum_{t=1}^{n} 2^t \text{ or with any other letter used for an index.}$$

6 - 7 : A basic rule of summation is

$$\sum_{k=1}^{n} (a_k + b_k) = \sum_{k=1}^{n} a_k + \sum_{k=1}^{n} b_k$$

Example:

$$\sum_{k=1}^{4} (2^k + k) = (2 + 1) + (4 + 2) + (8 + 3) + (16 + 4)$$

$$= 40$$

$$\sum_{k=1}^{4} 2^k + \sum_{k=1}^{4} k = (2 + 4 + 8 + 16) + (1 + 2 + 3 + 4)$$

$$= 40$$

What is $\sum_{p=1}^{3} (p^2 + 2^p)$?

$$\sum_{p=1}^{3} p^2 + \sum_{p=1}^{3} 2^p = (1 + 4 + 9) + (2 + 4 + 8) = 28$$

6 - 8 : An unusual looking sum is

$$\sum_{k=1}^{5} 2 = 2 + 2 + 2 + 2 + 2 = 10$$

What is $\sum_{n=1}^{4} (3 + n)$?

$$\sum_{n=1}^{4} 3 + \sum_{n=1}^{4} n = (3 + 3 + 3 + 3) + (1 + 2 + 3 + 4)$$

$$= 22$$

This could also be summed directly as $4 + 5 + 6 + 7 = 22$.

6 - 9 : Another property of summation is

$$\sum_{k=1}^{n} Ca_k = C \sum_{k=1}^{n} a_k$$

Example:

$$\sum_{k=1}^{3} 5k = 5 \sum_{k=1}^{3} k = 5(1 + 2 + 3) = 30$$

Evaluate $\sum_{k=1}^{4} 3k^2$.

———

$$\sum_{k=1}^{4} 3k^2 = 3 \sum_{k=1}^{4} k^2 = 3(1 + 4 + 9 + 16) = 90$$

———

6 - 10 : Here is a list of sums.   Cover the right side of each equation and see whether you can get the correct answer.

a: $\displaystyle\sum_{n=2}^{6} \frac{1}{2 + 4n} = \frac{1}{10} + \frac{1}{14} + \frac{1}{18} + \frac{1}{22} + \frac{1}{26}$

b: $\displaystyle\sum_{n=0}^{4} \frac{1}{10 + 4n} = \frac{1}{10} + \frac{1}{14} + \frac{1}{18} + \frac{1}{22} + \frac{1}{26}$

c: $\displaystyle\sum_{i=0}^{5} \frac{1}{i + 1} = 1 + \frac{1}{2} + \frac{1}{3} + \frac{1}{4} + \frac{1}{5} + \frac{1}{6}$

d: $\displaystyle\sum_{i=1}^{6} \frac{1}{i} = 1 + \frac{1}{2} + \frac{1}{3} + \frac{1}{4} + \frac{1}{5} + \frac{1}{6}$

e: $\displaystyle\sum_{i=0}^{5} \frac{1}{6 - i} = \frac{1}{6} + \frac{1}{5} + \frac{1}{4} + \frac{1}{3} + \frac{1}{2} + 1$

Notice that c, d, and e are all the same series.

f: $\displaystyle\sum_{k=1}^{3} k! = 1 + 1 \cdot 2 + 1 \cdot 2 \cdot 3 = 9$

g: $\displaystyle\sum_{h=0}^{5} \frac{h}{3+h} = 0 + \frac{1}{4} + \frac{2}{5} + \frac{3}{6} + \frac{4}{7} + \frac{5}{8}$

h: $\displaystyle\sum_{h=3}^{9} \frac{h+1}{h-1} = \frac{4}{2} + \frac{5}{3} + \frac{6}{4} + \frac{7}{5} + \frac{8}{6} + \frac{9}{7} + \frac{10}{8}$

6-11: The sequence $(0.3,\ 0.03,\ 0.003,\ 0.0003,\ \ldots,\ 3/10^n,\ \ldots)$ converges to 0, so it does not converge to $\frac{1}{3}$. We can construct a sequence from it, called a sequence of partial sums, which does converge to $\frac{1}{3}$.

Let

$s_1 = 0.3 = 0.3$

$s_2 = 0.3 + 0.03 = 0.33$

$s_3 = 0.3 + 0.03 + 0.003 = 0.333$

$\cdots \cdots \cdots \cdots \cdots \cdots \cdots \cdots$

$s_n = 0.3 + 0.03 + \cdots + \dfrac{3}{10^n} = 0.333 \cdots 3$

$(s_1,\ s_2,\ s_3,\ \ldots,\ s_n,\ \ldots)$ is a sequence of partial sums. Each s_n is a partial sum. The limit of this sequence is $\frac{1}{3}$.

$$\lim_{n \to \infty} (s_n) = \lim_{n \to \infty} \sum_{k=1}^{n} \frac{3}{10^k} = 0.333 \cdots = \tfrac{1}{3}$$

Construct a sequence of partial sums of the sequence $(0.2,\ 0.02,\ 0.002,\ \ldots,\ 2/10^n,\ \ldots)$.

$$\left(0.2,\ 0.22,\ 0.222,\ \ldots,\ \sum_{k=1}^{n} \frac{2}{10^k},\ \ldots \right)$$

DEFINITION 6-1:

Given the sequence $(a_n) = \{(n, y)|y = a_n$, where n is a natural number}, we can form another sequence

$$s_1 = a_1$$
$$s_2 = a_1 + a_2$$
$$s_3 = a_1 + a_2 + a_3$$
$$s_4 = a_1 + a_2 + a_3 + a_4$$
$$\cdot \cdot \cdot \cdot \cdot \cdot \cdot \cdot \cdot \cdot \cdot \cdot \cdot$$
$$s_n = a_1 + a_2 + a_3 + a_4 + \cdot \cdot \cdot + a_n$$

The sequence $(s_n) = \{(n, y)|y = \sum_{k=1}^{n} a_k$, where n is a natural number} is called the *sequence of partial sums* of the sequence (a_n). The *sum of the sequence* (a_n) is the limit of the sequence (s_n).

We shall define a closed interval before we define an integral. An interval is closed if it contains its end points. The neighborhoods we have been using throughout this study are open intervals. If we add the end points to an open interval, it becomes a closed interval. The neighborhood $N_1(5)$ does not contain the end points 4 and 6. Any point in this neighborhood has many other points of the neighborhood on both sides of it (like the *open* cattle range out West, it contains no fence). In a closed interval one can pick a point of the interval and say this is the right-hand boundary (like a fenced-in cattle range). The closed neighborhood $N_1^c(5)$ includes both the point 4 and the point 6. We can talk about the largest point in a closed interval, but we cannot talk about a largest point in an open interval.

Example:

$\{x|0 \le x \le 3\}$ is the closed interval [0; 3].
$\{x|0 < x < 3\}$ is the open interval (0; 3).

What is the largest point in the *open* interval $(4; 6) = N_1(5)$? There is no such point, but 6 is the largest point in the closed interval $[4; 6] = N_1^c(5)$. The smallest point in [4; 6] is 4, but there is no smallest point in (4; 6).

The concept of integration is an application of the limit which has been very useful in the calculus. When one integrates, one sums up a lot of little parts into a more meaningful whole.

Archimedes (287–212 B.C.) developed the method of *exhaustion* for computing the area of a circle. He inscribed a regular polygon, which we shall call $\underline{P}_n$, in the circle (see Fig. 6-1); then he circumscribed a regular polygon $\bar{P}_n$ having the same number of edges. The area of the inscribed polygon $\underline{P}_n$ is less than the area of the circle, which is less than the area of the circumscribed polygon $\bar{P}_n$. Since Archimedes knew how to figure the areas of $\underline{P}_n$ and $\bar{P}_n$ for any number n of sides, he could compute the area of a circle to

Figure 6-1

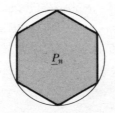
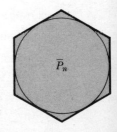

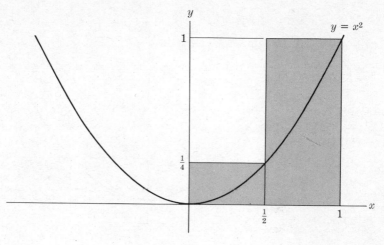

Figure 6-2

any degree of accuracy he wished by simply taking the time to calculate it.

We shall not compute the area of a circle, but we shall attack a similar problem of finding the area under a curve.

Suppose we have a graph of the equation $y = x^2$; what is the area under this curve from 0 to 1? To be more exact, what is the area bounded by the x axis, $x = 0$, $x = 1$, and $y = x^2$?

The area from 0 to 1 (A_0^1) is certainly less than the area (Fig. 6-2) of the set of rectangles obtained by dividing the interval [0; 1] into two subintervals [0; $\frac{1}{2}$] and [$\frac{1}{2}$; 1] and forming two rectangles using the heights at their right end points, $\frac{1}{4}$ and 1.

The area A_0^1 is greater than the area (Fig. 6-3) of the two rectangles formed from the subintervals [0; $\frac{1}{2}$] and [$\frac{1}{2}$; 1] with heights 0 and $\frac{1}{4}$ at their left end points. By

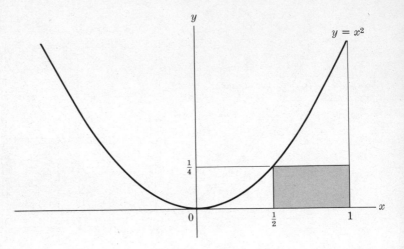

Figure 6-3

dividing the interval $[0; 1]$ into three (Figs. 6-4 and 6-5) equal subintervals, $[0; \tfrac{1}{3}]$, $[\tfrac{1}{3}; \tfrac{2}{3}]$, and $[\tfrac{2}{3}; 1]$, we obtain

$$0 + (\tfrac{1}{3})(\tfrac{1}{9}) + (\tfrac{1}{3})(\tfrac{4}{9}) = \tfrac{5}{27} \leq A_0^1 \leq \tfrac{14}{27}$$
$$= (\tfrac{1}{3})(\tfrac{1}{9}) + (\tfrac{1}{3})(\tfrac{4}{9}) + (\tfrac{1}{3})(1)$$

Figure 6-4

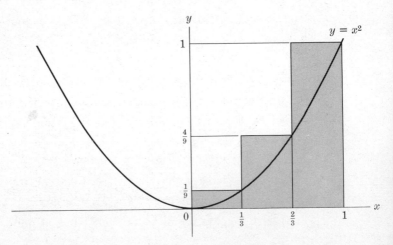

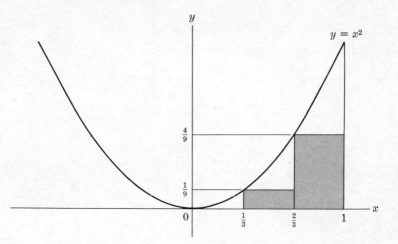

Figure 6-5

Four equal subintervals (Figs. 6-6 and 6-7) give

$$0 + (\tfrac{1}{4})(\tfrac{1}{16}) + (\tfrac{1}{4})(\tfrac{1}{4}) + (\tfrac{1}{4})(\tfrac{9}{16}) = \tfrac{7}{32} \leq A_0^1$$
$$\leq \tfrac{15}{32} = (\tfrac{1}{4})(\tfrac{1}{16}) + (\tfrac{1}{4})(\tfrac{1}{4}) + (\tfrac{1}{4})(\tfrac{9}{16}) + (\tfrac{1}{4})(1)$$

Figure 6-6

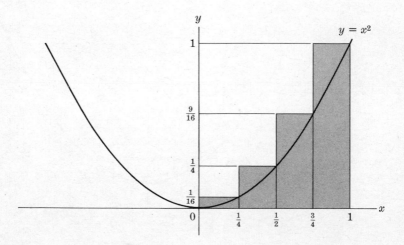

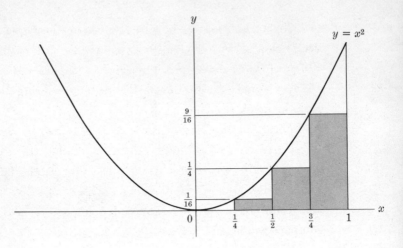

Figure 6-7

Figure 6-8

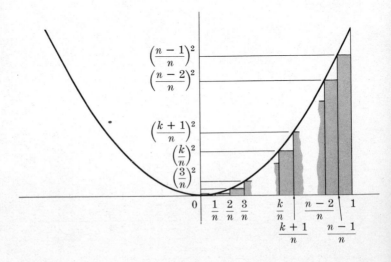

In fact, no matter how fine we make the bases of our rectangles, A_0^1 is less than or equal to the sum of the rectangles formed using the right sides as heights and greater than or equal to the sum of the rectangles using the left sides as heights.

Let $\underline{S}_n$ be the area (see Fig. 6-8) obtained by dividing $[0, 1]$ into n equal subintervals and summing the areas of the rectangles formed by using the height at the left end point of the subinterval forming its base. Let $\bar{S}_n$ be the area obtained using the right end point (see Fig. 6-9) to compute the height. Then, $\underline{S}_n \leq A_0^1 \leq \bar{S}_n$.

We can form two sequences:

$$(\bar{S}_n) = (1, \tfrac{5}{8}, \tfrac{14}{27}, \tfrac{15}{32}, \ldots, \bar{S}_n, \ldots)$$
$$(\underline{S}_n) = (0, \tfrac{1}{8}, \tfrac{5}{27}, \tfrac{7}{32}, \ldots, \underline{S}_n, \ldots)$$

Figure 6-9

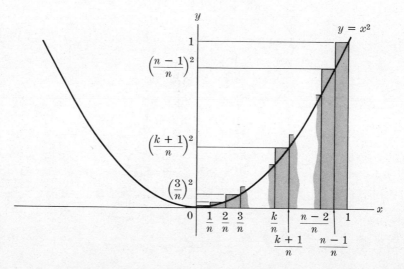

To find the limit of these sequences we shall investigate the behavior of the general terms of the sequences.

$$\underline{S}_n = 0 + \frac{1}{n}\left(\frac{1}{n}\right)^2 + \frac{1}{n}\left(\frac{2}{n}\right)^2 + \cdots + \frac{1}{n}\left(\frac{n-1}{n}\right)^2$$

$$= \frac{1}{n}\left(\frac{0+1}{n^2} + \frac{4}{n^2} + \cdots + \frac{(n-1)^2}{n^2}\right)$$

$$= \frac{1}{n}\frac{1}{n^2}(0 + 1 + 4 + \cdots + (n-1)^2)$$

But $1^2 + 2^2 + 3^2 + \cdots + k^2 = (k/6)(k+1)(2k+1)$ for k a natural number, so,

$$\underline{S}_n = \frac{1}{n^3}\frac{n}{6}(n-1)(2n-1) = \frac{(n-1)(2n-1)}{6n^2}$$

Likewise,

$$\bar{S}_n = \frac{1}{n}\left(\frac{1}{n}\right)^2 + \frac{1}{n}\left(\frac{2}{n}\right)^2 + \cdots + \frac{1}{n}\left(\frac{n-1}{n}\right)^2 + \frac{1}{n}\left(\frac{n}{n}\right)^2$$

$$= \frac{1}{n}\left(\frac{1}{n^2} + \frac{4}{n^2} + \cdots + \frac{(n-1)^2}{n^2} + \frac{n^2}{n^2}\right)$$

$$= \frac{1}{n^3}\frac{n}{6}(n+1)(2n+1) = \frac{(n+1)(2n+1)}{6n^2}$$

We are now in a position to calculate the area A_0^1 under the curve $y = x^2$ from 0 to 1:

$$\lim_{n\to\infty} \bar{S}_n = \lim_{n\to\infty} \frac{(n+1)(2n+1)}{6n^2}$$

$$= \lim_{n\to\infty} \frac{2n^2 + 3n + 1}{6n^2}$$

$$= \lim_{n\to\infty} \left(\frac{1}{3} + \frac{1}{2n} + \frac{1}{6n^2}\right)$$

$$= \lim_{n\to\infty} \frac{1}{3} + \lim_{n\to\infty} \frac{1}{2n} + \lim_{n\to\infty} \frac{1}{6n^2} = \frac{1}{3} + 0 + 0$$

$$\lim_{n\to\infty} \bar{S}_n = \frac{1}{3}$$

So the area $A_0^1 \leq \frac{1}{3}$. We will now figure the limit of the lower sum sequence

$$(0, \tfrac{1}{8}, \tfrac{5}{27}, \; \ldots \; , [(n - 1)(2n - 1)]/6n^2, \; \ldots)$$

We have

$$\lim_{n \to \infty} \underline{S}_n = \lim_{n \to \infty} \frac{(n - 1)(2n - 1)}{6n^2}$$

$$= \lim_{n \to \infty} \frac{2n^2 - 3n + 1}{6n^2}$$

$$= \lim_{n \to \infty} \frac{1}{3} + \lim_{n \to \infty} \frac{1}{2n} + \lim_{n \to \infty} \frac{1}{6n^2} = \frac{1}{3}$$

Now we have that

$$\tfrac{1}{3} \leq A_0^1 \leq \tfrac{1}{3}$$

therefore, A_0^1 is $\frac{1}{3}$.

In this example, the sequences $(\underline{S}_n)$ and $(\bar{S}_n)$ converge to the same limit, which is the area under the curve. In fact, if we form a sequence (S_n) of the sums of the areas of all the rectangles formed on equal subintervals by choosing any point x_i within each subinterval to determine the height $f(x_i)$ of the rectangle having that closed subinterval as a base, then the limit of this sequence will be the area under the curve. We shall use this observation in formulating our "definition" of the definite integral.

Consider a continuous function $\{(x, y) \,|\, y = f(x), x \in R\}$, defined on the closed interval $[a; b]$. We may divide the interval $[a; b]$ into n equal subintervals (Fig. 6-10) each of length $\Delta x = (b - a)/n$. We then form the sum

$$S_n = f(x_1) \, \Delta x + f(x_2) \, \Delta x + \cdots + f(x_{n-1}) \, \Delta x + f(x_n) \, \Delta x$$

$$= \sum_{i=1}^{n} f(x_i) \, \Delta x$$

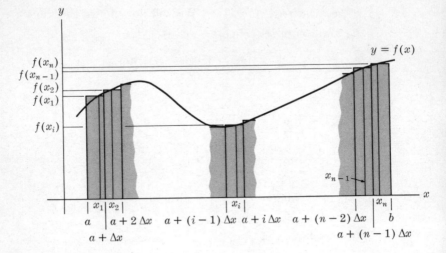

Figure 6-10

where x_i is in the ith subinterval,

$$a + (i - 1)\, \Delta x \leq x_i \leq a + i\, \Delta x$$

We are approximating the area under the curve in much the same way as we did in the examples, except that now we allow x_i to be any x value in the ith interval instead of simply the right or left end point.

The sums $S_n, n = 1, 2, 3, \ldots$, form a sequence $(S_1, S_2, S_3, \ldots)$. The limit of this sequence, $\lim_{n \to \infty} S_n$, is interpreted to be the definite integral of f from a to b and is symbolized $\int_a^b f(x)\, dx$. We shall not take the time to define the definite integral in a more complete manner, but we do believe that this "definition," which is based on the area under a curve, will aid the student in understanding the various definitions found in the calculus books.

When we are discussing positive functions which are continuous on the real domain and whose range is the set of real numbers, the definite integral can be interpreted to be the area under the curve, and we can write

$$A_a^b = \lim_{n \to \infty} S_n = \lim_{n \to \infty} \sum_{i=1}^{n} f(x_i)\,\Delta x = \int_a^b f(x)\,dx$$

where

$$\Delta x = \frac{b - a}{n}$$

and

$$a + (i - 1)\,\Delta x \le x_i \le a + i\,\Delta x$$

(see Fig. 6-10).

Another application of the limit concept is in finding the slope of a line tangent to a curve at a point $(x, f(x))$. If we graph a continuous function f, we obtain a smooth curve. We shall call a line "tangent to a curve" if it has the same slope as the curve at the point of tangency. In Fig. 6-11 we have graphed a tangent line along with several secant lines. In this graph the secant lines are those lines which cross the curve in two places. The tangent line touches the curve in only one point and has the same slope as the curve at this point.

Although it is obvious which of these lines is the tangent line, it is a bit difficult to tell exactly what its slope is. Suppose we wish to know the slope of the line tangent to the graph of the function $f = \{(x, y) | y = x^2\}$ at the point $(3, 9)$. In Fig. 6-12 we have graphed the tangent line and three secant lines. The first secant line passes through the point

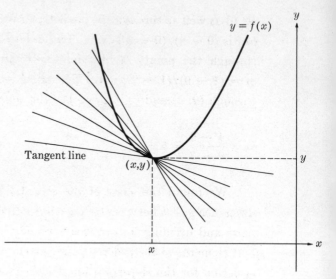

Figure 6-11

Figure 6-12

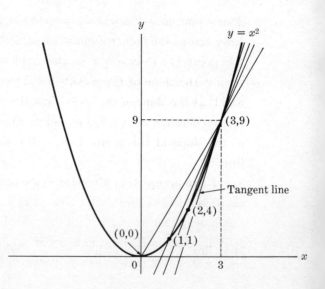

(0, 0) as well as through the point (3, 9), so the slope of that line is $(0 - 9)/(0 - 3)$, or 3.   The second secant line passes through the points (1, 1) and (3, 9) and has the slope $m = (1 - 9)/(1 - 3) = 4$.   The third secant line passes through (2, 4) and (3, 9), and has the slope

$$m = \frac{4 - 9}{2 - 3} = 5$$

We found the slope of the secant line by taking the difference $y - b$ between the second elements of the ordered pairs and dividing it by the difference $x - a$ between the first elements of the ordered pairs; we can therefore form an equation for the slope of a line passing through (x, y) and (a, b)

$$\text{Slope} = m = \frac{y - b}{x - a}$$

This equation will not work for the tangent line, however. If we accept the fact that the slope of the secant line through the point (1, 1) is closer to the slope of the tangent line than is the slope of the secant line through the point (0, 0) and that the slope of the secant line through the point (2, 4) is even closer, then we can postulate that the limit as $x \rightarrow 3$ of the slope of the secant lines is the slope of the tangent line.

If we accept this, then the slope of the tangent line at (3, 9) is

$$m = \lim_{x \to 3} \frac{f(x) - f(3)}{x - 3} = \lim_{x \to 3} \frac{x^2 - 3^2}{x - 3} = \lim_{x \to 3} x + 3 = 6$$

6-12 : By following this same type of reasoning, find the slope of the graph of $\{(x, y)|y = x^2\}$ at the point $(4, 16)$.

———

8, since $\lim\limits_{x \to 4} \dfrac{x^2 - 4^2}{x - 4} = \lim\limits_{x \to 4} x + 4 = 8$.

———

6-13 : What is the slope of the graph of $\{(x, y)|y = x^2\}$ at the point $(1, 1)$?

———

2, since $\lim\limits_{x \to 1} \dfrac{x^2 - 1^2}{x - 1} = \lim\limits_{x \to 1} x + 1 = 2$.

———

6-14 : If we assume that the same process will work with other functions, what is the slope of the tangent line to the curve $y = x^2 + x$ at the point $(3, 12)$?

———

7, since $\lim\limits_{x \to 3} \dfrac{(x^2 + x) - 12}{x - 3} = \lim\limits_{x \to 3} \dfrac{(x - 3)(x + 4)}{x - 3} = 7$.

———

This simple line of reasoning was a difficult concept for man to develop. The slope of the line tangent to the graph of a function is the *derivative* of that function evaluated at the point of tangency. We shall now state the usual definition of the derivative.

In Figure 6-13, we let $h = x - a$, and we let $f(a + h) - f(a)$ replace $f(x) - f(a)$; then the slope of the tangent line at a point $(a, f(a))$ takes the form

$$m = \lim_{h \to 0} \frac{f(a + h) - f(a)}{h}$$

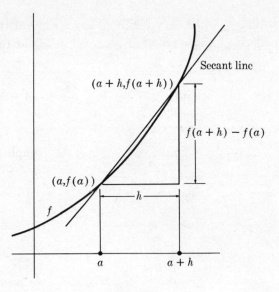

Figure 6-13

DEFINITION 6-2:

Let f be defined on the closed interval $[a; b]$. We say that f is *differentiable* at $x \in [a; b]$ if and only if

$$\lim_{h \to 0} \frac{f(x + h) - f(x)}{h}$$

exists. This limit is called "the derivative of f at x" and is denoted by $f'(x)$.

6-15: Let $f(x) = x^3 + 1$. Find the derivative of f at 2.

$f'(2) = 12$

since

$$f'(2) = \lim_{h \to 0} \frac{f(2 + h) - f(2)}{h}$$

$$= \lim_{h \to 0} \frac{(8 + 12h + 6h^2 + h^3 + 1) - (8 + 1)}{h}$$

$$= \lim_{h \to 0} \frac{12h + 6h^2 + h^3}{h}$$

$$= \lim_{h \to 0} 12 + 6h + h^2$$

$$= 12$$

6-16 : Let $f = \{(x, y) | y = 1/x, \; x \neq 0\}$.   Find $f'(5)$.

$f'(5) = -\frac{1}{25}$

since

$$f'(5) = \lim_{h \to 0} \frac{f(5 + h) - f(5)}{h}$$

$$= \lim_{h \to 0} \frac{1/(5 + h) - \frac{1}{5}}{h}$$

$$= \lim_{h \to 0} \frac{5 - (5 + h)}{5h(5 + h)}$$

$$= \lim_{h \to 0} \frac{-1}{25 + 5h}$$

$$= \frac{-1}{25}$$

6-17 : What is the slope of the line tangent to the curve $g(x) = x^2 + x + 1$ at the point $(-3, 7)$?

-5.   The slope of the tangent line at $(-3, 7)$ is simply $g'(-3)$.

$$g'(-3) = \lim_{h \to 0} \frac{g(-3 + h) - g(-3)}{h}$$

$$= \lim_{h \to 0} \frac{(7 - 5h + h^2) - 7}{h}$$

$$= \lim_{h \to 0} -5 + h$$

$$= -5$$

6-18 : Find the derivative of $f = \{(x, y)|y = x^2\}$ at a point x in its domain.

———

$f'(x) = 2x$

since

$$f'(x) = \lim_{h \to 0} \frac{f(x + h) - f(x)}{h}$$
$$= \lim_{h \to 0} \frac{(x + h)^2 - x^2}{h}$$
$$= \lim_{h \to 0} \frac{2xh + h^2}{h}$$
$$= \lim_{h \to 0} 2x + h$$
$$= 2x$$

Notice that we may use the equation $f'(x) = 2x$ to define a new function $f' = \{(x, y)|y = 2x\}$, which we call the *derivative* of f. The value of this function at any point b in its domain is $f'(b)$, the derivative of f at b.

———

6-19 : Let $g = \{(x, y)|y = x^3\}$. Find $g'(x)$.

———

$g'(x) = 3x^2$

since

$$g'(x) = \lim_{h \to 0} \frac{(x + h)^3 - x^3}{h}$$
$$= \lim_{h \to 0} \frac{x^3 + 3x^2h + 3xh^2 + h^3 - x^3}{h}$$
$$= \lim_{h \to 0} 3x^2 + 3xh + h^2$$
$$= 3x^2$$

———

6 - 20 : Let $k(x) = x^4$. Find $k'(x)$.

$k'(x) = 4x^3$

since

$$k'(x) = \lim_{h \to 0} \frac{(x + h)^4 - x^4}{h}$$

$$= \lim_{h \to 0} \frac{x^4 + 4x^3h + 6x^2h^2 + 4xh^3 + h^4 - x^4}{h}$$

$$= \lim_{h \to 0} 4x^3 + 6x^2h + 4xh^2 + h^3$$

$$= 4x^3$$

---

6 - 21 : Frames 6-7 to 6-9 show that

If $f = \{(x, x^2)\}$, then $f' = \{(x, 2x)\}$
If $g = \{(x, x^3)\}$, then $g' = \{(x, 3x^2)\}$ and
If $k = \{(x, x^4)\}$, then $k' = \{(x, 4x^3)\}$

This suggests that

If $p = \{(x, x^n)\}$, then $p' = \{(x, nx^{n-1})\}$

Show that this is the case if n is a positive integer. *Hint:*
If n is a positive integer, then by the binomial theorem,

$(x + h)^n = x^n + nx^{n-1}h + \frac{1}{2}n(n - 1)x^{n-2}h^2$
$+$ (a finite number of terms containing higher powers of h)

$$p'(x) = \lim_{h \to 0} \frac{p(x + h) - p(x)}{h}$$

$$= \lim_{h \to 0} \frac{(x + h)^n - x^n}{h}$$

$$= \lim_{h \to 0} \frac{(x^n + nx^{n-1}h + \frac{1}{2}n(n - 1)x^{n-2}h^2 + \cdots) - x^n}{h}$$

$$= \lim_{h \to 0} nx^{n-1} + \frac{1}{2}n(n - 1)x^{n-2}h + \cdots$$

Since all polynomials are continuous, we may substitute 0 for h. Consequently, all the terms are 0 except the first. Therefore,

$$p'(x) = nx^{n-1}$$

Hence,

$$p' = \{(x, nx^{n-1})\}$$

Although the derivative and integral have different histories and the definitions we have just given seem unrelated, they are linked by the following theorem:

If f and g are two functions continuous on the closed interval $[a; d]$ such that $f(x) = g'(x)$ for each x in $[a; d]$, then for any two points b and c in the interval $[a; d]$,
$$\int_b^c f(x)\ dx = g(c) - g(b)$$

This theorem relates differentiation and integration in such a way that they might almost be considered the inverse of each other.   The function f is the derivative of the function g at any point in the interval, and the integral of the function f from b to c is the difference $g(c) - g(b)$.

In coming to the conclusion of this study, we wish to define the derivative and integral without ever referring to limits.   Since it will be a self-contained derivation, we shall restate some definitions.

First we shall define continuity at a point b in the domain of a function from a subset of the real numbers into the real numbers.

DEFINITION I:

A function f is *continuous at a point* b in its domain if and only if

for each positive real number ε
there exists a positive real number δ
   such that
for each x in the domain of f
if $|x - b| < \delta$, then $|f(x) - f(b)| < \varepsilon$.

DEFINITION II:

A function is called a *continuous function* if and only if it is continuous at every point in its domain.

A function is *discontinuous* at a point in its domain if it is *not continuous* at that point. A function is certainly not continuous at points that are not in its domain, but we shall reserve the term *discontinuous* for points in the domain where the function is not continuous. We shall not discuss continuity at points not in the domain of the function.

DEFINITION III:

Let f and g be defined on the closed interval $[a; d]$. The function g is *tangent* to the function f at the point b in $[a; d]$ if and only if the function $h = \{(x, y)|y = |f(x) - g(x)|/|x - b|$ when $x \neq b$, $y = 0$ when $x = b\}$ is continuous at b.

DEFINITION IV:

Let f be continuous on the closed interval $[a; d]$. f is *differentiable* at a point b in $[a; d]$ if and only if there exists a real number u such that

$$g = \{(x, y)|y = f(b) + u(x - b)\}$$

is tangent to f at the point b. The real number u is called the *derivative* of f at the point b and is symbolized $f'(b)$.

DEFINITION V:

Let f be continuous on the closed interval $[a; d]$. A function g is an *antiderivative* of f on $[a; d]$ if and only if g is differentiable at all points x in the domain of f and $g'(x) = f(x)$.

DEFINITION VI:

Let f be continuous on the closed interval $[a; d]$. If g is any antiderivative of f, the difference $g(c) - g(b)$ for any two points b, c in $[a; d]$ is written $\int_b^c f(x)\,dx$ and is called the *integral* of f between b and c.

Another way to define the calculus from a foundation of continuity is to define the limit from continuity and then to define the derivative and integral in the standard way. We shall now define limit point and limit of a function using our definition of continuity at a point as a basis.

DEFINITION VII:

A point b is a *limit point* of the domain of f if and only if every deleted neighborhood of b contains at least one point of the domain of f.

DEFINITION VIII:

The real number L is the *limit* of $f(x)$ as x approaches the limit point b of the domain of f if and only if the function $g = \{(x, y) | y = f(x)$ when $x \neq b$, $y = L$ when $x = b\}$ is continuous at b.

Problem Set

Find the indicated limits:

1. $\lim\limits_{y \to 4} (4y - 3)$

2. $\lim\limits_{x \to 1} (x^2 - 3x + 5)$

3. $\lim\limits_{p \to 3} (2p^2 - p - 15)$

4. $\lim\limits_{x \to -1} (5x^3 + 3x^2 + 6x + 2)$

5. $\lim\limits_{\theta \to 2} \dfrac{2\theta}{\theta^2 + 4}$

6. $\lim\limits_{y \to 3} \dfrac{y + 3}{y + 2}$

7. $\lim\limits_{s \to 2} \dfrac{2s^2 + s + 5}{s - 1}$

8. $\lim\limits_{x \to 0} \dfrac{3x + 5x^2}{x}$

9. $\lim\limits_{k \to 0} \dfrac{k^3 + 4k^2}{k^2 + 5k}$

10. $\lim\limits_{x \to 0} \dfrac{x^5 + 8x^4 + 12x^3 + x^2 + 3x}{5x}$

11. $\lim\limits_{\alpha \to 2} \dfrac{\alpha^2 - 4}{\alpha - 2}$

12. $\lim\limits_{x \to -1} \dfrac{x^2 - 1}{x + 1}$

13. $\lim\limits_{t \to -4} \dfrac{t^2 - t - 20}{t + 4}$

14. $\lim\limits_{x \to 1} \dfrac{x^2 + 2x - 3}{x - 1}$

15. $\lim\limits_{x \to -3} \dfrac{x + 3}{x^2 + 7x + 12}$

16. $\lim\limits_{\beta \to 2} \dfrac{\beta^2 - 3\beta + 2}{\beta - 2}$

17. $\lim\limits_{y \to -3} \dfrac{y^2 + 4y + 3}{y + 3}$

18. $\lim\limits_{x \to 3} \dfrac{x^2 - 9}{x^2 - 2x - 3}$

19. $\lim\limits_{y \to 1} \dfrac{y^3 - 1}{y - 1}$

20. $\lim\limits_{x \to -2} \dfrac{x^3 + 8}{x + 2}$

21. $\lim\limits_{t \to 3} \dfrac{t^3 - 27}{t - 3}$

22. $\lim\limits_{p \to 1} \dfrac{p^2 + 2p - 3}{p^2 - 5p + 4}$

23. $\lim\limits_{x \to 0} \dfrac{1}{3x}\left(\dfrac{1}{8 + x} - \dfrac{1}{8}\right)$

24. $\displaystyle \lim_{x \to 0} \frac{1}{x^2} \left(\frac{2}{x-5} - \frac{2}{x^2+x-5} \right)$

25. $\displaystyle \lim_{x \to +\infty} \frac{3x+1}{8x+2}$

26. $\displaystyle \lim_{x \to -\infty} \frac{3x+1}{8x+2}$

27. $\displaystyle \lim_{x \to +\infty} \frac{x+1}{x^2+1}$

28. $\displaystyle \lim_{h \to +\infty} \frac{h+3}{3h^2-2}$

29. $\displaystyle \lim_{h \to +\infty} \frac{3h^2-2}{h+3}$

30. $\displaystyle \lim_{h \to -\infty} \frac{3h^2-2}{h+3}$

31. $\displaystyle \lim_{x \to +\infty} \frac{3x^2-6x}{8x^2+3}$

32. $\displaystyle \lim_{x \to +\infty} \frac{2x+12}{x^2+x+1}$

33. $\displaystyle \lim_{x \to -\infty} \frac{-x^2-3x+2}{5x^2+3x-1}$

34. $\displaystyle \lim_{x \to -\infty} \frac{5x^3+2x^2-7x+9}{9x^3-8x^2+9x-16}$

35. $\displaystyle \lim_{x \to -\infty} 3^{1/x}$

36. $\displaystyle \lim_{y \to +\infty} \frac{y-1}{2-2^{1/y}}$

37. $\displaystyle\lim_{x \to +\infty} \frac{12^{1/x}}{x}$

38. $\displaystyle\lim_{x \to 0} 2x \cos x$

39. $\displaystyle\lim_{\alpha \to 0} \frac{\sin x}{5x}$

40. $\displaystyle\lim_{k \to 0} \frac{\sin 5k}{k}$

41. $\displaystyle\lim_{x \to 0} \frac{\sin (4x/5)}{x}$

42. $\displaystyle\lim_{y \to 0} \frac{\sin 5y}{\sin y}$

43. $\displaystyle\lim_{t \to 0} \frac{\sin^2 t}{t}$

44. $\displaystyle\lim_{t \to 0} \frac{\sin^2 t}{t^2}$

45. $\displaystyle\lim_{x \to +\infty} \int_1^x \frac{dt}{t^2}$

46. $\displaystyle\lim_{s \to 0} \frac{\tan s}{s}$

47. $\displaystyle\lim_{\theta \to (\pi/2)+} \tan \theta$

48. $\displaystyle\lim_{\theta \to (\pi/2)-} \tan \theta$

49. $\displaystyle\lim_{\alpha \to \pi/2} \frac{\cos \alpha}{\pi/2 - \alpha}$

50. $\displaystyle\lim_{\theta \to \pi/2} \left(\frac{\pi}{2} - \theta\right) \tan \theta$

51. $\lim\limits_{h \to 0} \dfrac{\sqrt{3 + h} - \sqrt{3}}{h}$

52. $\lim\limits_{h \to 0} \dfrac{\sqrt[3]{3 + h} - \sqrt[3]{3}}{h}$

53. $\lim\limits_{x \to 1} \dfrac{x^2 - 1}{\sqrt{x^2 + 3} - 2}$

54. $\lim\limits_{x \to 3} \dfrac{x^2 - 9}{\sqrt{x^2 + 7} - 4}$

55. $\lim\limits_{x \to -1} \dfrac{4 - \sqrt{x^2 + x + 16}}{x^3 + 1}$

56. $\lim\limits_{x \to 0} \dfrac{x^2 - 3x + 5}{2x - 7}$

Answers to Problems

1.	13	29.	$+\infty$
2.	3	30.	$-\infty$
3.	0	31.	$\frac{3}{8}$
4.	-6	32.	0
5.	$\frac{1}{2}$	33.	$-\frac{1}{5}$
6.	$\frac{6}{5}$	34.	$\frac{5}{9}$
7.	15	35.	1
8.	3	36.	$-\infty$
9.	0	37.	0
10.	$\frac{3}{5}$	38.	0
11.	4	39.	$\frac{1}{5}$
12.	-2	40.	5
13.	-9	41.	$\frac{4}{5}$
14.	4	42.	5
15.	1	43.	0
16.	1	44.	1
17.	-2	45.	1
18.	$\frac{3}{2}$	46.	1
19.	3	47.	$-\infty$
20.	12	48.	$+\infty$
21.	27	49.	1
22.	$-\frac{4}{3}$	50.	1
23.	$-\frac{1}{192}$	51.	$\frac{1}{2}\sqrt{3}$
24.	$\frac{2}{25}$	52.	$\frac{1}{3}\sqrt[3]{3^2}$
25.	$\frac{3}{8}$	53.	4
26.	$\frac{3}{8}$	54.	8
27.	0	55.	$\frac{1}{24}$
28.	0	56.	$-\frac{5}{7}$

Appendix: Sets, Inequalities, and Absolute Values

DEFINITION A-1:

Let x be any real number.   Then

$|x| = x \qquad$ **if $x > 0$**

$|x| = -x \qquad$ **if $x < 0$**

$|x| = 0 \qquad$ **if $x = 0$**

Property A-1: Properties of Inequalities:

If a, b, and c are real numbers, then

1: $\quad a < b \Rightarrow a + c < b + c$

2: $\quad a < b, c > 0 \Rightarrow ac < bc$

3: $\quad a < b, c < 0 \Rightarrow ac > bc$

THEOREM A-1:

For any real numbers x and y,

i) $\quad |x| \geq 0$

ii) $\quad |x| \geq x$

iii) $\quad |x| \geq -x$

iv) $\quad |xy| = |x|\,|y|$

v) $\quad |x + y| \leq |x| + |y|$

vi) $\quad |x - y| \geq |x| - |y|$

Proof:

iv) *Case 1: $xy \geq 0$.* Then both $x \geq 0$ and $y \geq 0$, or both $x \leq 0$ and $y \leq 0$. In the former instance, $|x| = x$ and $|y| = y$, so that $|x|\,|y| = xy$. In the latter instance, $|x| = -x$ and $|y| = -y$, whence

$$|x|\,|y| = (-x)(-y) = xy$$

But since $xy \geq 0$, $xy = |xy|$, so we have $|xy| = |x|\,|y|$ for case 1.

Case 2: $xy < 0$. Then either $x < 0$ with $y > 0$, or $x > 0$ with $y < 0$. In the first instance, $|x| = -x$, $|y| = y$, and $|x|\,|y| = -xy$. In the second instance, $|x| = x$, $|y| = -y$, and $|x|\,|y| = x(-y) = -xy$. But since $xy < 0$, $|xy| = -xy$. Therefore, $|xy| = |x|\,|y|$ for all x and y.

v) *Case 1: $x + y \geq 0$.* Then $|x + y| = x + y$. From (ii), $|x| \geq x$ and $|y| \geq y$, so that

$$|x| + |y| \geq x + y = |x + y|$$

Case 2: $x + y < 0$. Then $|x + y| = -(x + y)$. From (iii), $|x| \geq -x$ and $|y| \geq -y$, so that

$$|x| + |y| \geq -x - y = -(x + y) = |x + y|$$

Therefore, $|x + y| \leq |x| + |y|$ for all x and y.

vi) *Case 1: $x \geq 0$.* Then $|x| = x$. Also, from (ii), $|y| \geq y$, which is the same as $-|y| \leq -y$. This gives $|x| - |y| \leq x - y$. But by (ii), $x - y \leq |x - y|$. Hence $|x - y| \geq |x| - |y|$ for this case.

Case 2: $x < 0$. Then $|x| = -x$. Also, from (iii), $|y| \geq -y$, which is the same as $-|y| \leq y$. This gives $|x| - |y| \leq -x + y = -(x - y)$. But by (iii), $-(x - y) \leq |x - y|$. Therefore, we conclude that $|x - y| \geq |x| - |y|$ for all x and y.

THEOREM A-2:

If $|x - y| < c$, then $y - c < x < y + c$ and conversely.

Proof: First assume that $|x - y| < c$. By (ii) of Theorem A-1, $|x - y| \geq x - y$, so that $x - y < c$. By (iii) of the same theorem, $|x - y| \geq -(x - y)$, so that $-(x - y) < c$, which is the same as $x - y > c$. Thus we have $-c < x - y < c$, from which it follows that $y - c < x < y + c$.

To prove the converse, assume that $y - c < x < y + c$. Then $-c < x - y < c$. If $x - y > 0$, then

$$|x - y| = x - y$$

so that $|x - y| < c$. If $x - y < 0$, then $-|x - y| = x - y$, so that $-c < -|x - y|$, which is the same as $|x - y| < c$.

Therefore, $|x - y| < c$ is equivalent to $y - c < x < y + c$.

DEFINITION A-2:

The *open interval* $(a; b)$ is defined to be $\{x | a < x < b\}$. The open interval from a to b is defined to be the set of all real numbers x such that x is between a and b.

DEFINITION A-3:

The *closed interval* $[a; b]$ is defined to be $\{x | a \leq x \leq b\}$ The closed interval from a to b is defined to be the set of all real numbers x such that x is greater than or equal to a and less than or equal to b.

A-1: $|x| < 2$ can be written $|x - 0| < 2$; by Theorem A-2 this becomes $0 - 2 < x < 0 + 2$, which is the same as saying that $x \in N_2(0)$ or that $x \in (-2; 2)$. If $|x| < 5$, then we

can write $|x - 0|$ _____. This becomes _____ $<$ _ $<$
_____ by Theorem A-2, which is the same as saying that
$x \in N$ ( ) or that $x \in$ (;).

___

If $|x| < 5$, then we can write $|x - 0| < 5$. This becomes $0 - 5 <$
$x < 0 + 5$ by Theorem A-2, which is the same as saying that
$x \in N_5(0)$ or that $x \in (-5; 5)$.

___

A-2: If $|x - 3| < 2$, then we can write $3 - 2 < x < 3 + 2$
because of Theorem A-2, which is also written $x \in N_2(3)$,
or x is in the open interval $(1; 5)$. If $|x - 3| < 1$, then we
can write _____ $<$ _ $<$ _____ because of Theorem A-2.
We can also write $x \in N$ ( ) or $x \in$ (;).

___

If $|x - 3| < 1$, then we can write $3 - 1 < x < 3 + 1$ because
of Theorem A-2. We can also write $x \in N_1(3)$ or $x \in (2; 4)$.

___

A-3: If $x \in N_{1/2}(6)$, then _____ $< x <$ _____ and $|x - \_| < \_$.
Also, x is in the open interval $(11\frac{1}{2}; 13\frac{1}{2})$.

___

If $x \in N_{1/2}(6)$, then $6 - \frac{1}{2} < x < 6 + \frac{1}{2}$ and $|x - 6| < \frac{1}{2}$.

___

A-4: If $|x + 3| < 1$, then $x \in N_1(-3)$ and _____ $< x <$ _____.

___

$(-3) - 1 < x < (-3) + 1$

___

A-5: If $|x + 2| < 1$, then x is in the open interval (;).

___

$(-3; -1)$

___

A - 6 : Given the statement $|x - 5| < 1$, we can show that $|x - 4| < 2$.

Given:

$|x - 5| < 1$

$4 < x < 6$ by Theorem A-2

$4 - 4 < x - 4 < 6 - 4$ by Property A-1

$0 < x - 4 < 2$

$|x - 4| < 2$ this step is not reversible

So $|x - 5| < 1 \Rightarrow |x - 4| < 2$. This should not be surprising since $4 < x < 6$ implies that $2 < x < 6$. Start with the statement $|x - 5| < 1$ and prove that $|x + 4| < 10$.

Proof:

$|x - 5| < 1$

$4 < x < 6$ by Theorem A-2

$4 + 4 < x + 4 < 6 + 4$ by Property A-1

$|x + 4| < 10$

A - 7 : Derive $|x + 1| < 8$ from $|x + 8| < 1$.

$|x + 8| < 1 \Rightarrow -9 < x < -7 \Rightarrow -9 + 1 < x + 1 < -7 + 1$
$$\Rightarrow -8 < x + 1 < -6 \Rightarrow |x + 1| < 8$$

The manipulations of the past few frames play a very important part in the proofs in Chap. 3. We shall now turn to a discussion of open and closed intervals, which play such an important part in our discussion of the domains of piecewise functions.

DEFINITION A-4:

$A \cup B = \{x | x \in A \text{ or } x \in B\}$

The union of set A and set B is defined to be the set of all x such that x is an element of A or x is an element of B.

DEFINITION A-5:

$A \cap B = \{x | x \in A \text{ and } x \in B\}$

The intersection of set A and set B is defined to be the set of all x such that x is an element of A and x is an element of B.

A-8: We shall write $(-\infty; a)$ for the set of all real numbers less then a, and $(a; +\infty)$ for the set of all real numbers greater than a; that is $(-\infty; a) = \{x | x < a\}$ and

$(a; +\infty) = \{x | x > a\}$

If $|x| > 6$, then x could be in $(-\infty; -6)$ or in $(6; +\infty)$. This means that $x < -6$ or $x > 6$. The symbolism $x \in (-\infty; -6) \cup (6; +\infty)$ is read "x is in the union of the open interval from minus infinity to -6 and the open interval from 6 to positive infinity." If $|x| > 5$, then x is an element of $(\ ;\ ) \cup (\ ;\ )$.

_____

$(-\infty; -5) \cup (5; +\infty)$

_____

A-9: If $|x| > 6$, then x is *not* in the closed interval $[-6; 6]$. If x is in $[-6; 6]$, then x is in the set $\{x | -6 \leq x \leq 6\}$. If $|x| > 5$, then x is not in the closed interval $[\ ;\ ]$.

_____

$[-5; 5]$

_____

A - 10 : If $x > 5$ or $x < -5$, then $|x|$ _____.

$|x| > 5$

A - 11 : If $|x| = 5$, then x is in the set _____.

$\{5, -5\}$. That is, x is 5, or x is -5.

A - 12 : In review:

If $|x| = 4$, then x is in $\{\quad\}$.
If $|x| < 4$, then x is in $(\ ;\ )$.
If $|x| > 4$, then x is in $(\ ;\ ) \cup (\ ;\ )$.
If $|x| \leq 4$, then x is in $[\ ;\ ]$.
If $|x| \geq 4$, then x is in $(\ ;\ ] \cup [\ ;\ )$.

$\{4, -4\}$	x is 4 or x is -4
$(-4; 4)$	$-4 < x < 4$
$(-\infty; -4) \cup (4; +\infty)$	$x < -4$ or $x > 4$
$[-4; 4]$	$-4 \leq x \leq 4$
$(-\infty; -4] \cup [4; +\infty)$	$x \leq -4$, or $x \geq 4$

A - 13 : If the domain of the function f is defined to be the set of all x such that $x > 2$ and $x < 5$, then the domain of the function $D_f = (2; +\infty) \cap (-\infty; 5)$, which is the open interval $(2; 5)$. What is the domain of a function g, if x is in D_g when $x > 1$ and $x < 5$?

$D_g = (-\infty; 5) \cap (2; +\infty) = (2; 5)$

A - 14 : If the domain of a function f is the set of all x such that $3 \leq x \leq 5$ or $x > 13$, what is the set on which it is defined?

$D_f = [3; 5] \cup (13; +\infty)$

A-15: The function represented by the equation

$$y = \frac{x - 3}{(x + 2)(x - 3)}$$

has what domain in the real numbers?

$(-\infty; -2) \cup (-2; 3) \cup (3; +\infty)$

A-16: What is the domain of the function represented by the following equation?

$$y = \frac{x - 3}{x(x - 4)}$$

$(-\infty; 0) \cup (0; 4) \cup (4; +\infty)$

Index